WHITE STAR LINE

In Picture Postcards

WHITE STAR LINE

In Picture Postcards

Robert McDougall and Robin Gardiner

CONTENTS

Picture Credits

All the pictures reproduced in this book are from Robert McDougall's collection unless credited otherwise.

Ship Names and Tonnages

White Star reused a number of older ships' names for new vessels at various times. Whenever confusion might arise these are distinguished in the text as in the following example: *Adriatic*[1] (launched 1871, scrapped 1899) and *Adriatic*[2] (entered service 1907, scrapped 1934).

All ship tonnages are given as gross register except where noted otherwise, where they follow the format in which they are listed in the records. Other measurements likewise follow the format in which they are listed in the records.

Front cover: **clockwise from top left: 1920s poster, *Olympic* interior, *Oceanic*[2], *Olympic*.**

Back cover: **clockwise from top left: *Majestic*[2], poster, *Adriatic* souvenir postcard, *Dawpool*.**

For further information on the White Star Line and its vessels the following titles from Ian Allan Publishing may be of interest:

The History of the White Star Line, ISBN 0 7110 2809 5
Titanic: The Ship That Never Sank, ISBN 0 7110 2777 3
Titanic in Picture Postcards, ISBN 0 7110 2896 6
Who Sailed on Titanic: The Definitive Passenger Lists, ISBN 0 7110 2880 X

First published 2003

ISBN 0 7110 2986 5

Published by Ian Allan Publishing

an imprint of Ian Allan Publishing Ltd, Hersham, Surrey KT12 4RG.
Printed by Ian Allan Printing Ltd, Hersham, Surrey KT12 4RG.

Code: 0308/B2

INTRODUCTION

The story of the White Star Line begins in 1845 with the partnership between Henry Threlfall Wilson and John Pilkington, when they set themselves up as shipbrokers. In February 1846 they chartered their first ship, the brig *Elizabeth*. The partnership prospered and three years later they bought a ship of their own, the 879grt *Iowa*. June 1849 saw the first advertised sailing by a vessel of the 'White Star Line of Boston Packets' appear in the Liverpool newspapers.

Gold was discovered in Australia in 1851 and Wilson and Pilkington were quick to see the potential profit in the hordes of would-be prospectors heading for the antipodes. They quickly advertised sailings by the *Bhurtpoor*, *Blanche*, *Dundonald* and *Phoenix* for the new gold-fields. The 978-ton *Bhurtpoor*, intended to inaugurate the new service, was wrecked off the coast of Ireland, near Wexford, and was replaced by the 397-ton *Ellen*, which sailed on 23 July 1852.

Left: **This advertised sailing of the US-built *Red Jacket* dates from 1865, the very early days of the White Star Line when Henry Threlfall Wilson and John Cunningham operated sailing vessels between Liverpool and Melbourne. The Native American portrayed is Chief Sagoyewatha of the Seneca tribe. His habit of wearing a red jacket with a five-pointed white star on the front provided the inspiration for the ship's name, the name of the line and the famous house flag of a white star on a red background.**

Just over a year later the partners chartered the full-rigged, 1,997-ton iron ship *Tayleur*, named after her builder, from Moore & Co, who had bought her specifically to charter to White Star. The maiden voyage of the *Tayleur* was another first for the White Star Line, but unfortunately not a last. The *Tayleur* left Liverpool on Thursday 19 January 1854. The weather was atrocious as the ship battled her way southwards down the Irish Sea. At about 11.30am on the 20th the *Tayleur* crashed into Lambay Island, about 15 miles northeast of Dublin. The heavy seas pounded the ship to pieces as passengers and crew fought to reach the safety of the island. Almost two thirds of them failed. About 250 people survived the wreck, while another 420 died. With the loss of the *Tayleur*, the White Star Line gained the dubious distinction of holding the record for the worst shipping disaster in history to date, for the first time.

In the same year as the *Tayleur* disaster a new apprentice started work for the shipbroking firm of Imrie, Tomlinson & Co, of Liverpool. He was the 16-year-old Thomas Henry Ismay and within a short time he had befriended William Imrie, the son of a partner in the firm employing him. In time, Ismay and Imrie would become partners and do more to influence the fortunes of the White Star Line than possibly anybody else, with the exceptions of Ismay's son, Joseph Bruce Ismay, and the American financier, John Pierpont Morgan.

Early in 1854 Pilkington and Wilson bought the extreme clipper *Red Jacket*. The ship's figurehead was a carving of a North American Indian wearing a red jacket with a large five-pointed white star on the breast, the design adopted for the White Star Line's house flag.

At the end of 1856 John Pilkington left the partnership with Henry Wilson to return to his family's glass-producing business. To take his place Wilson took on another partner, his brother-in-law, James Chambers. This partnership also went well and in 1863 Wilson and Chambers bought their first steamship, the *Royal Standard*. Speed of passage was the greatest attraction for fare-paying passengers. Whichever line could boast the fastest ships on the Australian route would attract the greatest numbers of passengers. With this in mind, Henry Wilson had always restricted his charters to the fastest sailing vessels around, and he had despatched those vessels lightly loaded with cargo to enable them to make the fastest passages possible. But in 1863 he went too far, at least where James Chambers was concerned, when he guaranteed, under penalty, that his ships would make the voyage from Liverpool to Melbourne in 68 days. Chambers was so alarmed by Wilson's guarantee, and his own potential liability as a partner, that he resigned on the last day of the year.

In the meantime, Thomas Ismay had married Margaret Bruce. They were to have six daughters, two of whom died young, and three sons. The eldest son, Joseph Bruce Ismay, was born on 12 December 1862. T. H. Ismay had taken on a partner, Philip Nelson, a few years before, principally because Nelson already owned a small ship, the *Angelita*. Like Wilson and Chambers, Ismay was now in the shipping business as part owner of his own ship. In 1863 Nelson retired and Ismay changed the company name from Nelson, Ismay & Co to T. H. Ismay & Co. A year later Ismay became a director of the National Line, which had been set up to trade specifically with the southern states of America, better known as the Confederacy, during the Civil War. With this in mind, all of the ships belonging to the line had been named after Confederate states. Even as Ismay joined the National Line the war between the states was raging and the Confederates were losing. The decisive battle of Gettysburg had been fought over the first three days of June the previous year. Inevitably, the names of the ships belonging to the National Line had to be changed before the company could serve the Union port of New York.

In 1865 Henry Threlfall Wilson took on yet another partner, John Cunningham. Wilson and Cunningham, as the partnership was known, tried desperately to take advantage of the increased demand for passage to Australia brought about by the gold rush. They expanded their fleet, with the aid of loans, far too rapidly, and by the autumn of 1867 owed the Royal Bank of Liverpool the enormous sum of £527,000. They had no hope of repaying the loans and two years later, in 1869, were forced into liquidation. The partners' ships were sold off to repay their creditors. The White Star name, the house flag, whatever goodwill still attached to the White Star company and the famous red burgee with its five-pointed white star were also put up for sale. The name, flags and goodwill were snapped up by Thomas Henry Ismay for the not inconsiderable sum of £1,000.

Ismay had an ambition to own and operate the finest fleet of steamships engaged in the lucrative North Atlantic trade. All he needed was financial backing, and he knew where to find that.

While having dinner with Gustavus Schwabe, a Liverpool financier, in 1869, Ismay put forward his ideas. Schwabe's nephew, Gustav Wilhelm Wolff, was a junior partner in the Belfast shipbuilding company, Harland & Wolff. Schwabe immediately saw that if Ismay's new shipping line bought all of its vessels from Harland's, the yard would have a guaranteed income. With this in mind he offered to finance Ismay and to persuade other financiers to do the same. An agreement was reached: Ismay would have all of his ships built at the Belfast yard on a cost plus profit basis, which would ensure that the builders constructed the very best ships possible. In return for this guarantee of work the shipyard would, in turn, refrain from building vessels for any of Ismay's competitors.

Ismay would have the finest ships in the world, and Harland & Wolff would have no worries about having to build to contract prices or that the company might show a loss on any vessel constructed on Ismay's instructions. (With the exception of the second *Laurentic*, all of the ships were built on this basis.) The White Star Line, as it is remembered, or Oceanic Steam Navigation Company to give it its proper title, was born.

Above: **A very early example of the White Star Line logo.**

Left: **Thomas Henry Ismay, who bought the White Star name and flag in 1869 and began to use steamships between Liverpool and the USA.**

A NEW AGE OF TRAVEL

On 6 September 1869 the Oceanic Steam Navigation Company (OSN Co) was registered with capital amounting to £400,000, in £1,000 shares, with its offices at 10 Water Street, Liverpool. Of these, Thomas Ismay and his general manager, George Hamilton Fletcher, each held 50. Gustavus Schwabe held another 12.

Almost immediately an order was placed with Harland & Wolff for four radical new steamers, designed by Edward Harland and George Fletcher, specially for the North Atlantic trade. The order was soon increased to six ships, all to be built using only the finest materials and workmanship and to be paid for on the 'cost plus agreed profit' basis. With the signing of this initial contract, Edward Harland and Gustav Wolff both became shareholders in the OSN Co.

Harland had a revolutionary new idea about ship design. Instead of building a hull, putting on the top deck and then building passenger quarters on top of that, he proposed that the hull sides should continue up to form the sides of the passenger accommodation, thus avoiding the necessity for deckhouses. The new ships would not have individual deckhouses as every passenger vessel before them had, but all the deckhouses would be joined together and extended out to the sides of the hull. What would have been open decks adjoining passenger cabins and public rooms on earlier ships were roofed over with relatively lightweight iron sheeting, forming what is now known as a promenade deck. Even the solid bulwark, pierced by scuppers, had gone, to be replaced by open railings so that any wave that should break over the decks was soon cleared away. This new class of vessel would be the first to have a superstructure that would be instantly recognisable to a modern eye. The White Star steamers built on this principle would, at a stroke, render all previous passenger vessels obsolete.

In 1870 William Imrie, Ismay's old friend from his days as an apprentice, became a partner in the company and the name was changed to Ismay, Imrie & Co. Imrie would concentrate on the sailing ships which the company still owned, leaving Ismay free to focus on the new steamers. The very first White Star liner, Harland & Wolff yard No 73, *Oceanic*[1] named after the shipping company, slid down the slipway into the River Lagan on 27 August. She was 420ft long, 40ft wide and weighed in at 3,707 gross register tons.

The public had grown used to the idea that White Star operated sailing ships on the Liverpool to Australia run. Its whole concept of

Right: **The maiden voyage of *Oceanic*[1] was in 1871. She was the first of a series of similar vessels constructed by Harland & Wolff following the founding of the Oceanic Steam Navigation Company, better known as the White Star Line.**

the White Star Line must have been altered by the advertisement that appeared in the *Liverpool Daily Post* on 1 March 1871:

> **'WHITE STAR LINE, OCEANIC STEAM NAVIGATION CO LTD**
> The new first-class, full-powered screw steamships *Oceanic*, *Baltic*, *Atlantic*, *Pacific*, *Arctic*, *Adriatic*.
> Sailing on Thursdays from Liverpool, and calling at Queenstown on Fridays to embark passengers.
> Will sail as under for New York, via Queenstown. *Oceanic*, 4,500 tons, 3,000 H.P., Capt Digby Murray, to sail to-morrow, Thursday, March 2nd, 1871.'

Fares, by the standards of today, appear to be ridiculously low. First class passage cost £18 18s 0d or £16 16s 0d, and a return ticket cost 27 guineas. Steerage price was as low as with any other first-class line of the time.

Oceanic[I] set out from Liverpool on her maiden voyage to New York on 2 March 1871. No sooner had she departed than problems with the 1,990hp engines forced her to return to port; the maiden voyage was abandoned. It was not an auspicious start for the new White Star Line. After repairs *Oceanic*[I] tried again on the 16th, this time more successfully. So successfully, in fact, that satisfied passengers declared her to be the finest vessel on the North Atlantic. Nevertheless, she was not popular with the public at large, despite being fitted throughout with electric lights, running water to first class cabins and push buttons to summon stewards. After only four years she was chartered to the Occidental & Oriental Steam Ship Company for use on a new service between San Francisco, Yokohama and Hong Kong.

The second of Ismay's new liners, *Atlantic*, was launched on 1 December 1870. In practically all respects she was the same size, layout and specification as her sister, *Oceanic*[I], but unlike her she was an immediate success with the travelling public. On 8 June 1871 *Atlantic* set out on her maiden voyage from Liverpool to New York, via Queenstown in Ireland.

The advent of the new large steamers in 1871 brought an old problem to a head. Liverpool had long been a very busy port, with many ships jockeying for berths. Because of its intention to run a regular weekly service Ismay, Imrie believed that it was high time that the Docks and Quays Committee set aside pier space for it. After some discussion the committee initially offered White Star space on the south side of the Morpeth Dock, but Ismay wanted something better. Eighteen months after the committee's initial offer Ismay got his way in the form of a permanent berth for White Star steamers in the West Waterloo Dock of some 2,772sq yd.

The third of the new liners was not slow in arriving from the builders, and she sailed on her maiden voyage in September 1871. Originally planned as the *Pacific*, she was renamed *Baltic*[I] while still in the stocks when it was recalled that a Collins Line vessel of that name had disappeared in 1856.

Ever since the days of Nelson, Ismay & Co, Ismay had run sailing ships to South America. With the advent of the new steamships he began to wonder if a changeover to steam on that route as well might be advantageous. He despatched an agent, Henry Griffin, to South America to find out if there was an opening for steamships trading with countries there. Griffin was back within the year to report that there was indeed an opportunity. As a result of Griffin's report, Ismay, Imrie bought two steamships from J. M. Wood for use in the South Atlantic trade: the 2,652-ton *Asiatic*[I] and the 2,650-ton *Tropic*[I].

Accidents were only to be expected with these revolutionary new vessels. *Atlantic* left the Mersey on 30 November 1871, bound for New York, via Queenstown. Half an hour later the Inman liner *City of Paris* also left Liverpool.

For whatever reason the *Atlantic* had been instructed to keep the speed down until she reached the open sea, with the result that at about 5pm she was overhauled by the *City of Paris*. No sooner had the Inman liner overtaken the White Star vessel than she suddenly turned to port, cutting across the bows of the White Star ship, a mere 50 to 60yd away. As both ships were travelling at somewhere between 10 and 12kt this was much too close for comfort, and the *City of Paris* was almost run down.

T. H. Ismay wrote to Inman's on the subject of reckless navigation, on 8 December 1871, saying: 'We have enjoined the masters and officers under our charge, to act on all occasions even in excess of mere prudence to avoid the possibility of danger.' As we shall see, captains not only disregarded this enjoiner but seem to have regarded it as a personal insult to their abilities.

Republic[I], the fourth of Ismay's new breed of liner, sailed on her maiden voyage early in 1872. Captain Digby Murray, who had taken each of the new class on its first run across the Atlantic, was not very impressed with the ships. They took aboard large quantities of seawater in anything approaching rough weather, which flooded crew quarters, passenger cabins and public rooms.

Another of the '*Oceanic*' class ships, the *Adriatic*[I], was launched on 17 October 1871. Although more spacious than *Oceanic*[I],

Below: **A cigarette card showing *Adriatic*[I]. Another liner in the '*Oceanic*' class, she took the record for the fastest westbound Atlantic crossing on her maiden voyage in 1872.**

Adriatic had a capacity of only 1,150 passengers, 1,000 of them in steerage. She sailed on her maiden voyage on 11 March 1872. The ship set a new east-to-west Atlantic record at an average speed of 14.52kt in June 1872.

White Star had received complaints from steerage passengers about conditions aboard its ships so Ismay, Imrie began changing the layout of third class accommodation. Until then third class passengers aboard steamers had traditionally been accommodated aft, where they had to put up with noise and vibration caused by the engines and propellers. Under Ismay's direction the shipping line began moving steerage quarters forward and higher up, away from the machinery. Married couples were provided with their own accommodation instead of sharing dormitories for 20 to 30 people. White Star also abolished the practice of third class passengers providing their own beds, bedding and eating utensils. The improved conditions brought more passengers to the line, forcing other lines to follow suit.

On 18 October the newly completed *Celtic*[1], having just been handed over to her new owners, ran aground as she was steaming down Belfast Lough. Originally it had been planned to call the vessel *Arctic* but the name was changed to *Celtic*[1] when it was pointed out to Thomas Ismay that a Collins Line vessel of that name had sunk in a collision in 1854. *Celtic*[1] made her maiden voyage for the White Star Line a little later in October. She was an almost exact duplicate of her sister ship *Adriatic*[1]. This practice of building more than one vessel from what was effectively the same set of plans was a very efficient means of cutting construction costs. It also meant that many of the line's vessels were practically indistinguishable from one another.

In December, during a westbound Atlantic crossing, *Adriatic*[1] ran into a particularly severe storm in which she lost two of the four blades of her single propeller. As Captain Hamilton Perry nursed his crippled vessel towards New York he came across the sailing ship *Allan*, which had been severely damaged and was sinking. *Adriatic* managed to save 20 crewmembers from the sailing vessel.

On All Fools' Day 1873 the White Star Company again became the holder of a dubious record, for the worst shipping disaster in history at that time. Twelve days before, on Thursday 20 March, *Atlantic* left Liverpool on her 19th and last voyage with about 967 tons of mixed Welsh and Lancashire coal in her bunkers, under the command of Captain James Agnew Williams, aged 33. Under normal conditions the vessel used about 58 tons of coal a day so she had enough aboard for slightly more than 16½ days' steaming. On her previous 18 voyages the longest time she had taken for a crossing had been 13 days and 10 hours, and her best time was 10 days and three hours, so there should have been no problems over the quantity of coal aboard.

Atlantic stopped at Queenstown to pick up a few more passengers and then set out to cross the North Atlantic. Aboard the vessel officially were just 32 first class and 767 steerage passengers, plus 143 crewmembers. There were also 14 stowaways aboard, making 956 in all. Of these people possibly as many as 200 were children.

Top: **Another, somewhat later, view of *Britannic*[1] taken at Liverpool shortly before she went to the breaker's in 1903.**

Above: **A cigarette card showing *Britannic*[1].**

By Tuesday the 25th *Atlantic* was battling against a full southwesterly gale, which slowed her down to about 8kt. By the following day the vessel had suffered a considerable amount of damage and her speed had been further reduced to about 5kt.

After 11 days at sea *Atlantic* was still 460 miles away from New York. Then the Chief Engineer, Foxley, reported that only enough coal remained in the bunkers to get them to within 80 miles of their destination. Captain Williams altered course for Halifax, Nova Scotia, some 170 miles away, where the ship could obtain additional coal and provisions.

At just before a quarter past three on the morning of 1 April, Joseph Carroll, a forward lookout, cried 'Breakers ahead!' The vessel struck Marr's Rock, about 50yd from Meagher's Island, Newfoundland, and heeled over to port. The Atlantic was 12 to 13 miles west of where the officers thought she was. Within seconds the heavy seas began to tear the ship apart and panic set in amongst the passengers.

One after another the port-side lifeboats were smashed to splinters or washed away by the waves. On the starboard side the crew struggled to lower the boats but the vessel listed over until this became impossible. As the list increased dozens of people were swept off the deck by the merciless waves. Water poured into the hull through every opening, drowning those persons who were still below decks.

At 6.30am local fishing boats began to arrive on the scene and to pick up survivors from the wreck. Amongst them was Captain

Above: **An 1874 advertising poster showing the *Britannic*[1], which entered service with the White Star Line in that year.**

Above right: Germanic **entered service with White Star in 1875. Despite being sunk twice, once in 1899 in New York harbour after icing up badly and again after being torpedoed in 1915, this vessel lasted longer than any other ship built for the White Star Line, finally going to the breaker's in 1950 after a career spanning 75 years.**

Right: **An early cigarette card showing *Germanic*.**

Williams, whose hair had, overnight, begun to turn white. One of the last two rescuees was the only child to survive the disaster. Of the unknown number of women who had taken passage on the vessel, not a single one survived. In the worst merchant shipwreck up to that time 565 men, women and children had perished.

Later in 1873, the 2,652-ton *Gaelic*[1] was purchased, being bought on the stocks from the owners of the Bibby Line. She turned out to be one of the line's more fortunate vessels and she served White Star for a decade without serious mishap.

A new 5,004-ton vessel, designed by Edward J. Harland, was launched at Belfast on 3 February 1874. The ship was originally to be called *Hellenic* but the name was changed to *Britannic*[1] before she was handed over to the White Star Line. It was not uncommon for White Star to change a vessel's name from time to time. *Britannic* quickly set new records for both east- and westbound Atlantic crossings.

White Star also bought the *Belgic*[1] in 1874. The new ship had been built as the *Gaelic* but as the line already had a vessel of that name an alternative had to be found.

Germanic, built at a cost of £200,000, entered service in 1875. Despite one or two quite spectacular mishaps, *Germanic* was to become White Star's longest-lived liner, lasting for no less than three-quarters of a century (albeit not all in White Star service). Along with the *Britannic*[1], she was considerably larger than the other vessels in the White Star fleet at the time.

In February 1876 the *Germanic* set a new record for an eastbound crossing of the North Atlantic when she completed the trip in 7 days, 15 hours and 17 minutes, at an average speed of 15.79kt. The same vessel later set a new record for a westbound North Atlantic crossing, in April 1877, when she completed the voyage in 7 days, 11 hours and 37 minutes, at an average speed of 15.76kt. She then held the record for both east and west passages.

By 1880 White Star was one of the most successful lines operating on the North Atlantic. T. H. Ismay had risen to eminence with his shipping line and he was also a director of the London & North Western Railway and the Royal Insurance Company, and on the board of governors of the Seaman's Orphanage and the training ship *Indefatigable*. Thomas Henry Ismay and his wife were pillars of the local community.

T. H. Ismay's eldest son, Joseph Bruce, completed his schooling in 1880 and on 13 September of that year he began his apprenticeship with Ismay, Imrie. Joseph Bruce Ismay had been educated at New Brighton, Elstree and Harrow, before being sent, at the tender age of 16, to a private tutor at Dinard, in France.

White Star was still taking delivery of new, and improved, vessels from Harland & Wolff. The *Arabic*[1] entered service with the line in 1881, followed by the new *Coptic*.

Right:* The *Dawpool* was an iron-hulled barquentine specially built for T. H. Ismay and his partner, William Imrie, in 1880. *Sea Breezes, September 1972

On 25 June 1881 the *Britannic*[1] departed New York bound for Queenstown and Liverpool. After a brief stopover at Queenstown *Britannic* set off on the last leg of the journey, only to encounter heavy fog. At about half past seven on the morning of 4 July, Captain Perry heard the Hoots fog signal (a gun fired every 10 minutes) and somehow mistook it for the signal from Tuskar Light (a gun fired every five minutes), so he altered course towards what he thought was Holyhead. *Britannic* was, in fact, somewhere off Killmore, County Wexford, Ireland. A few moments later the vessel ran hard aground.

The Liverpool Salvage Association soon had men on the scene and they set to work, pumping the water out of the ship and patching her up. Over the next day or so, 1,500 tons of cargo were removed from the holds and taken to Waterford. On 8 July, sufficiently lightened, *Britannic*[1] lifted off the bottom and was once again afloat but as she was being towed towards Liverpool she sprang another leak and began to sink. She was towed to South Bay and beached. By 12 July she was afloat again and on her way to Liverpool to be dried out.

During the early 1880s Ismay and Imrie decided to put a couple of steamers on the Australian route. As the Shaw Savill & Albion line had a vast amount of experience on this run it would make an ideal manager for Ismay, Imrie's new ships. An agreement was soon reached whereby the White Star Line would supply vessels and their crews, while Shaw Savill & Albion would arrange passengers, cargoes and schedules. With these new services in mind, two new ships were ordered from Harland & Wolff, the *Ionic* and the *Doric*[1].

Both the *Ionic* and the *Doric*[1] were specially built for the antipodean trade and were developments of the earlier '*Oceanic*' class ships. These two vessels were unparalleled at the time because they were the first ships built by the Belfast shipbuilders from steel instead of iron. They were each capable of transporting about 70 first class passengers. In one of his first public appearances for the line, the young J. Bruce Ismay joined the *Ionic* at Belfast on 26 March 1883, as she was being handed over by the builders, and made the trip from there to London, which was to be the home port for ships engaged on the antipodean run.

Doric[1] was completed and ready for delivery to the White Star Line early in July 1883 so on the 6th T. H. Ismay journeyed to Holyhead to join the vessel for the trip round to London from Belfast. *Coptic* set out on the first trip of the new White Star service from London to Hobart, Australia, on 26 May 1884.

Late in October 1884, J. Bruce Ismay sailed for New Zealand aboard the *Doric*[1]. The young Ismay had slightly less than a year to go to complete his apprenticeship and his father thought that it was time that he saw a little bit of the world for himself. In December of the same year *Ionic* joined *Coptic* and *Doric* on the new route from London to Australia and New Zealand.

With the new year of 1885 came a couple of new ships for the White Star Line. One of them was a vessel of 4,211 tons, to replace the old *Belgic*. In his characteristic way, T. H. Ismay had the new ship named *Belgic*[2]. The second vessel to come from the builders in 1885 was the 4,205-ton *Gaelic*[2] and both of the new ships were intended for the Australia and New Zealand route rather than the North Atlantic passenger trade.

In April 1885 *Germanic* was forced by exceptionally heavy seas and tremendous gales to abandon a westbound Atlantic crossing. This was the first time in the company's history that a White Star ship had been forced to return to port because of bad weather. The huge waves had severely damaged passenger accommodation and public rooms, and had smashed or carried away the lifeboats.

By 1887 it was felt that the White Star fleet was getting a bit long in the tooth and T. H. Ismay decided it was necessary to build some new ships. However, he did not want to spend any more of his or his shareholders' money than he could possibly avoid.

He suggested to the Admiralty that, with Government backing, new ships, which could be easily turned into armed merchant cruisers in the event of war, should be built under Admiralty supervision. The Government agreed and Edward Harland started designing two such vessels. In March 1887 the first keel, *Teutonic*, was laid, closely followed by that of *Majestic*[1].

The new liners were another breakthrough in technology for Edward Harland. They were the first modern twin-screw liners, and were designed to be able to complete a voyage under steam alone. The ships were to be of about 10,000 tons apiece and capable of 20kt.

On 11 May 1887 *Celtic*[1] departed Liverpool, bound for New York, with 104 first class and 765 steerage passengers aboard. Commanding *Celtic* was Captain Peter J. Irvine. A week later, on 18 May, *Britannic*[1], under the command of Captain Hamilton Perry, left New York, bound for Liverpool, with 176 first class and 300 steerage passengers. On Thursday 19 May both vessels encountered fog.

Britannic[1] was steaming through the thick fog during the afternoon of 19 May. Captain Perry was steaming at a speed he considered reasonable given the prevailing weather conditions, $14\frac{1}{2}$kt, or full ahead. At about a quarter past five a whistle was heard. *Britannic* changed course two points ($22\frac{1}{2}°$) to starboard and Captain Perry ordered the whistle sounded at one-minute intervals.

Celtic[1] had been steaming through the fog on a roughly reciprocal course to *Britannic*[1] at a speed Captain Irvine considered appropriate for the prevailing conditions, $13\frac{1}{2}$kt, or full ahead. Captain Irvine heard a ship's whistle about three points off his starboard bow, but ignored it. About five minutes later he heard the whistle again and ordered a course change of a point and a half (almost 17°) to starboard and the engine revolutions reduced. In an era renowned for robust captaincy, Captain Irvine was clearly nothing like as robust as Captain Perry. (A new fourth officer, E. J. Smith, who had joined *Celtic* in 1887 at the start of his service with the White Star Line, would turn out to be one of the most robust skippers of them all. He was to captain the *Titanic* on her fateful voyage.)

Both vessels reduced speed as they approached one another. Although *Celtic*[1] reversed her engines at the last moment, her bow struck the port side of the *Britannic*[1] abaft the mizzenmast, tearing a gap 4ft wide in her side at the waterline.

***Above: Majestic[1]* (1889), at the Empress Dock, Southampton in about 1907. She is the vessel tied up on the right.**

Britannic's No 4 hold was holed and quickly filled with water. Three of her lifeboats had been smashed and deckhouses had been damaged. Four of *Britannic's* steerage passengers had been killed in the collision and nine more were severely injured.

Britannic's passengers were transferred to the slightly less damaged *Celtic[1]* while carpenters set about patching the hole in her side. By midnight they had managed to do so sufficiently well to halt the incoming water but the vessel had settled about 5ft deeper than usual in the water.

Celtic[1] was in little better condition but her carpenters managed to shore up the forward bulkheads and keep her afloat. Soon after midnight both vessels were able to get under way.

It was in the next year, 1888, that J. Bruce Ismay first met his future bride, Florence Schieffelin, the eldest daughter of Mr and Mrs George Schieffelin, who were members of one of the oldest and most respected families in New York. The Schieffelins were not happy about the idea of their daughter going to live in England and it was only because Ismay promised that the couple would remain in America that the relationship was allowed to continue. J. Bruce and Florence were married on 4 December 1888, at the Church of the Heavenly Rest, New York. Despite his promise to Mr and Mrs Schieffelin to always live in America, Joseph Bruce Ismay and Florence arrived in Liverpool, aboard the *Adriatic[1]* on 22 December 1888, where they were met aboard by T. H. Ismay.

On 8 December, while J. Bruce Ismay was still in America, the new *Cufic[1]* began her maiden voyage. She was the first White Star ship to be fitted with triple-expansion steam engines. Her sister ship *Runic* joined the fleet early the following year.

On 20 February 1889 J. Bruce Ismay and his wife returned to New York aboard the *Germanic*. Once there he rented a house, 444 Madison Avenue, which suggests that he did not plan to stay there for too long.

Some time in 1889 Thomas Henry Ismay was, rather ironically as later events were to prove, elected chairman of the Board of Trade Lifesaving Appliances Committee. Five years later that same committee would lay down regulations covering the number of lifeboats a new passenger vessel must have, based on the tonnage of the ship. Those regulations, that did not envisage a vessel of more than 10,000 tons, would remain in effect for almost 20 years.

Following her trials in July 1889, *Teutonic*, which had been designed to serve the Royal Navy as an armed merchant cruiser in the event of war, sailed to the Mersey where eight 4.7in quick-firing guns were fitted in just 24 hours. A review of the fleet at Spithead had been arranged for 3 August 1889, and *Teutonic* was to be one of the star attractions as the first armed merchant cruiser.

Because of bad weather the fleet review was postponed for two days, until Monday 5 August. However, on the Sunday the Prince of Wales and his nephew, Kaiser Wilhelm, visited the *Teutonic* to inspect her. The German Emperor was very impressed with the ship, and remarked to the Prince of Wales: 'We must have some of these.'

Two days later, having had her guns removed, *Teutonic* was ready for her maiden voyage to New York and left Liverpool on 7 August. She reached Sandy Hook in the early hours of 15 August 1889, after a passage lasting 6 days, 14 hours and 20 minutes, during which she had encountered her fair share of rough weather.

A little later, in 1891, *Teutonic* would take the Blue Riband, awarded to the vessel making the fastest Atlantic crossing, and hold it for just two months. This was the last time a White Star ship was to hold, or even attempt to take, the record for the fastest Atlantic crossing. Instead, the company would rely on having the largest and most comfortable vessels to attract customers.

On 1 January 1891 both Joseph Bruce and his younger brother James Ismay were made partners in the firm of Ismay, Imrie. Exactly a year later T. H. Ismay officially retired from the firm of Ismay, Imrie and Company, although he remained as chairman and took an active part in the running of the company.

Gothic, ordered the year before from Harland & Wolff, was handed over to her new owners in November 1893. Specially designed for the London–New Zealand trade, she was the largest ship, at 7,755 tons, ever to have entered the Port of London up to that time. Thousands of people came to see the new ship and wish her well when she set off on her maiden voyage to Wellington on 30 December. Within a short time she had broken the speed records for both the outward and return trips by averaging better than 14kt.

In 1895 the six-year-old *Runic*[1] was sold to the West India & Pacific Steamship Company for £37,500, and renamed *Tampican*.

R.M.S. Teutonic
Length, 565 ft.
Breadth, 51 ft.
Tonnage, 9,984

Below: **RMS *Teutonic* (1889), the first White Star vessel to be designed for conversion into an armed merchant cruiser in the event of war.**

Right: **RMS *Teutonic* at Prince's Landing Stage, Liverpool, c1908.**

***Right:* Majestic[1] is seen at New York in about 1903.**

***Below:* Autographed portrait photograph of Thomas Henry Ismay, taken in 1892.**

She was transferred in 1899 to Frederick Leyland & Company and then sold in 1912 to H. E. Moss & Company, of Liverpool, and almost immediately sold again to the South Pacific Whaling Company of Oslo and renamed *Imo*. As the *Imo*, *Runic* almost went out with a bang when, on 12 June 1917, she ran into the French ammunition ship *Mont Blanc* at Halifax, Nova Scotia. The *Mont Blanc* exploded, killing about 1,500 people and injuring about another 8,000. A large part of the city of Halifax was destroyed in the blast. The *Imo*, unsurprisingly, was badly damaged in the incident and had to be beached to prevent her from sinking. In 1920 she was sold to Norwegian owners and renamed *Guvernoren*. On 30 November 1921 she was wrecked near Port Stanley in the Falkland Islands.

On Christmas Eve 1895 word reached the Ismays, as they all gathered at Dawpool, Thomas' house in the Wirral, for the season, that Sir Edward Harland had died suddenly. Sir Edward's funeral was on 28 December and T. H. Ismay made the journey to Belfast in order to attend. Harland and Ismay had been friends for 25 years and the White Star Line owed a lot of its success, as well as some of its hardships, to the vessels that had come from the Harland & Wolff Yard.

The year 1896 saw the White Star's very first liner, *Oceanic*[1], sent for scrap.

The next year, 1897, was the 60th year of Queen Victoria's reign, and in her honour another review of Her Majesty's ships at Spithead was scheduled. Once again *Teutonic* was armed to the teeth, ready to appear as an armed merchant cruiser. With 170 guests aboard, she sailed for Spithead. The review took place on Saturday 26 June 1897. The weather was perfect.

The big hit of the review was undoubtedly the *Turbinia*. This rather unusual-looking vessel arrived at Spithead uninvited and proceeded to pass back and forth through the lines of warships at incredible speeds, sometimes reaching 32kt. The reason behind the strange behaviour of the *Turbinia* was simple. The inventor of a new type of turbine engine, the Honourable Charles Parsons, was determined to show off its potential in a way that the Royal Navy could not ignore.

After its display of speed and agility the little *Turbinia* tied up alongside the *Teutonic* and Thomas Henry and J. Bruce Ismay were invited aboard, along with a guest, Sir George Baden Powell, to take a demonstration run.

On 31 December 1897 the Oceanic Steam Navigation Company moved offices from 10 Water Street to new purpose-built offices at 30 James Street, Liverpool, designed by Norman Shaw.

Things were going along quite smoothly in 1898, and it was time for another new ship to join the line, the 13,096-ton *Cymric*.

Harland & Wolff had for some time been working on the design of two new super-liners for White Star. The first of these ships was to be called the *Oceanic*[2] and the second, which was not actually built, was to have been *Olympic*. The name was not issued until 12 years later.

The magnificent new *Oceanic*[2], built by Harland & Wolff, was launched on 14 January 1899. T. H. Ismay and his wife had made the trip to Belfast for the launching and stayed with the Pirries. William James Pirrie had taken over as head of the Harland & Wolff on Edward Harland's retirement in 1895. Mrs Ismay described the event in her diary: 'A most beautiful sight it was to see the noble ship, glide so gracefully into the water.'

Afric, *Medic* and the slightly larger *Persic* all followed from Harland & Wolff, one after another. The new ships were specially designed for use on the Australian run. Although Harland & Wolff built the best ships it possibly could for White Star, it did not always get everything right. Following her maiden voyage in 1899, which was rather surprisingly to New York, *Afric* was returned to the builders for seven months of alterations and improvements.

Not long after the launching of the *Oceanic*[2], T. H. Ismay began to complain of pains in his chest. Despite the best efforts of his own doctor, and several others, Thomas's condition continued to deteriorate. In August 1899 he collapsed and was confined to bed as the *Oceanic* steamed majestically into the Mersey. He was too sick to accompany the new vessel on her maiden voyage, even

though he wanted to. However, he insisted on going aboard the new ship, and on 26 August he did so, remaining aboard for about three-quarters of an hour. The effort seems to have been too much for him and by the 28th he was seriously ill again.

S. S. Cymric (Twin Screw) 13096 Tons Length 585 1/2 ft., Breadth 64 1/3 ft.
WHITE STAR LINE
ROYAL & UNITED STATES MAIL STEAMERS
LIVERPOOL TO NEW YORK EVERY WEDNESDAY,
CALLING AT QUEENSTOWN EVERY THURSDAY.
Saloon Passage £10 and upwards according to Steamer Season & Accommodation.
Second Saloon Passage. £7 10/- and upwards according to Steamer Season & Accommodation.
3RD CLASS PASSAGE AT LOW RATES.
ISMAY, IMRIE & CO. LIVERPOOL
GREAT NORTHERN RAILWAY.

On 13 September 1899 T. H. Ismay had a heart attack, followed by several more occurring at intervals until 23 November. He died at about five minutes past six o'clock that evening. The death of Thomas Henry Ismay marked the end of an era as far as the White Star Line was concerned.

As the new century began, Joseph Bruce Ismay took control of the line, with the assistance of his brother James and two of his father's oldest friends and partners, William Imrie and W. S. Graves.

WHITE STAR LINE

"OCEANIC" LEAVING NEW YORK

Charles Dixon

Top left: Cymric (1898).

Bottom left: Persic (1899). She was designed specially for the Australia route.

Centre left: A White Star advertisement from about 1900 showing the *Oceanic*[2].

Above: Oceanic[2] (1899) arriving at Liverpool.

Left: Oceanic[2] leaving New York.

WHITE STAR
LINE.
"AFRIC" LEAVING MELBOURNE

WHITE STAR
LINE.
TWIN-SCREW S.S. "MEDIC,"
12,222 TONS.

Above left: Afric (1899), a sister ship of the *Persic*.

Left: Medic (1899). Although the second-built of the trio of liners specially designed for the Australia run, she was the first actually to sail to the antipodes.

Top: An official White Star postcard from *Oceanic*[2] (1899)

Above right: Persic at sea.

Right: Persic arriving at Sydney.

S.S. Oceanic.

CELEBRATED LINERS.
OCEANIC
S.S. OCEANIC.

***Above left: Oceanic*[2] was the largest ship in the world when she entered service in 1899.**

***Left: Oceanic*[2] at sea.**

***Above: Majestic*[1].**

***Top right:* Another official White Star postcard, which would have been available aboard *Majestic*[1].**

***Centre right: Majestic*[1] tied up at the landing stage, Liverpool.**

***Right: Cymric* at Boston, USA.**

Top: Majestic[1] at sea.

Above: Two White Star liners: the SS *Cufic* (1888) (left) and SS *Romanic* (1899) (right) taking on coal in the Mersey, in about 1900.

Right: The entrance to the Prince's Dock, Liverpool. The main terminal for Atlantic liners was located at the dock.

Top right: The White Star–Dominion Line vessel *Canada* (1896). This ship, which was built for the Dominion Line, served under White Star management as a troopship during the Boer War.

Far right: Another postcard showing the White Star–Dominion Line *Canada*.

S.S. Canada

WHITE STAR-DOMINION
LINE.
TWIN-SCREW S.S. "CANADA
9.472 TONS

Above right: The South Western Hotel, Southampton, which was the preferred hotel for the White Star Line's passengers departing from the Hampshire port.

Right and Below: Liverpool's London & North Western (right) and Adelphi (bottom) hotels, where many White Star passengers stayed overnight before joining their ships. The hotels were owned by the London & North Western Railway Company, of which the Ismays were major shareholders.

AN ANGLO-AMERICAN ALLIANCE

Although *Afric*, *Medic* and *Persic* were all designed from the outset for the Australian trade, the first to be used on that route was the second one built, *Medic*. The new ships were unusual in that they carried only third class passengers, who had the full run of the vessel. *Medic* left Liverpool on 3 August 1899 on her maiden voyage. Aboard *Medic* as her fourth officer was one Charles Herbert Lightoller, making his first voyage for the White Star Line. He would later play a significant part in the *Titanic* disaster. *Afric*, *Medic* and *Persic* were very successful so plans for two additional ships went ahead, although they would be a little larger than the first three, by about 500 tons.

Britannic[1] was declared surplus by OSN on her return from America in late August 1899. Almost immediately she was requisitioned by the British Government for use as a troopship for the Boer War. Under the designation *Transport Number 62* the *Britannic* made her first trip from Queenstown to South Africa on 26 October. In all she made 11 trips to South Africa and back, mostly from Southampton.

On 22 December 1900 *Runic*[2], the first of the two new, slightly enlarged, Australian-run vessels to follow *Afric*, *Medic* and *Persic*, was delivered to the White Star Line.

The last of the five vessels specially designed for the Australian run, *Suevic*, joined the White Star fleet on 9 March 1901. Before the line could make any use of the new vessel, however, she was immediately requisitioned by the British Government for use as a troopship.

On 4 April 1901 the first of what are known as the 'Big Four' liners was launched at Belfast. The *Celtic*[2], of 20,904 tons, was the last ship T. H. Ismay had ordered before his death. Until then the White Star Line had specialised in building ships that could carry very large cargoes as well as a great many passengers. The *Celtic*[2] was a new departure inasmuch as she was a passenger liner first and a cargo vessel second. Although she could carry 17,000 tons of general cargo, this was regarded as ballast to steady the ship in rough weather. The *Celtic* was an immediate success, many passengers preferring her extra steadiness to the slightly faster passages offered by other ships. The White Star Line promptly ordered another similar vessel, the *Cedric*.

By 1901 many shipping lines were struggling to make ends meet. Waiting in the wings for just this situation was the American financier John Pierpont Morgan. He began by buying up the American Line and then the Red Star, Dominion, Atlantic Transport and Leyland lines, in order to form the combine International Mercantile Marine (IMM). The ships of the IMM lines continued to sail under their own house and national flags because under American law only ships actually built in America could fly the Stars and Stripes. Having swallowed up the small fry, Morgan turned next to the major Atlantic passenger lines, Cunard, White Star, Hamburg-Amerika and Norddeutscher Lloyd.

He failed to buy the two German lines, and Cunard, with Government assistance, also managed to fight off the takeover. Cunard offered to build, with a Government subsidy, two new super-liners. These would be constructed in such a way as they could easily be converted into armed merchant cruisers in the event of war. The ships, which did not come into service for another five years, were the *Lusitania* and *Mauretania*, and they were to be followed shortly thereafter by a third sister, *Aquitania*. Cunard also undertook not to sell out to the Americans for at least 25 years, for an additional subsidy of £150,000 a year.

It had always been a policy of Morgan to offer more for a company than it appeared to be worth when he moved to take it over. He offered White Star's

***Left:* Joseph Bruce Ismay, T. H. Ismay's son, who took control of the line on the death of his father in 1899.**

shareholders 10 times as much as the line earned in 1900, which had been an exceptionally good year because the British Government had been obliged to charter so many ships for Boer War service.

Seventy-five percent of the shareholders wanted to accept Morgan's offer as it would give them a substantial profit on their original investments. Even James Pirrie, J. Bruce Ismay's friend, was for selling out, if only because he confidently expected all of the lines making up IMM to come to him for any new vessels. Morgan clinched the deal when he offered to keep Ismay on as managing director and chairman of the White Star Line.

By the time the takeover was agreed only two of the original partners in the Oceanic Steam Navigation Company were to remain with IMM and White Star: Joseph Bruce Ismay and Harold Sanderson. Ismay and Sanderson had become friends in 1886. In 1895 Ismay had invited Sanderson to join Ismay, Imrie & Company, and he was made a partner in 1900.

By May 1902 agreement had been reached and on the 17th of that month the last Annual General Meeting of the Oceanic Steam Navigation Company took place. Five days later the agreement between John Pierpont Morgan and the White Star Line was signed. All of the shareholders had been paid by the 1 December 1902 and the White Star Line belonged to J. P. Morgan as part of the IMM Group.

Above: Athenic **(1901), built for White Star's Australian service.**

Right: Athenic **was one of White Star's longest-lived vessels, only going to the breaker's in 1962.**

Centre right: Corinthic **(1902). She was a sister ship to *Athenic* and *Ionic*.**

Bottom right: Ionic² **(1903).**

Below: Suevic **(1901).**

F. T. Series No. 8340A
S.S. " Athenic," 12,234 tons

WHITE STAR
LINE.
TWIN-SCREW R.M.S. "CELTIC,"
21,026 TONS.
MONTAGUE BLACK.

46
THE LANDING STAGE, LIVERPOOL. S.S. CELTIC.

WHITE STAR LINE.
S.S. CEDRIC
TUCK'S POST CARD
CARTE POSTALE
POSTKARTE
(FOR ADDRESS ONLY.)
By Appointment.
CELEBRATED LINERS — "WHITE STAR LINE."
Raphael Tuck & Sons' "OILETTE" Postcard 9215.
ART PUBLISHERS TO THEIR MAJESTIES THE KING & QUEEN.
S.S. Cedric. One of the three largest vessels of the White Star fleet. Launched in 1902, at which time it was the largest boat in the world. Runs between Liverpool and New York. Tonnage 21,0 681 ft. long 75½ ft. broad Speed 17 knots.
Jan 5 - 1910
Printed in England

Above left: Celtic[2] – the first of the 'Big Four' liners.

Left: Celtic[2] at Liverpool.

Above and right: An official White Star postcard from *Cedric* with a handwritten message from J. Bruce Ismay, penned in 1910.

Bottom right: John Pierpont Morgan, the American banker and financier who set up International Mercantile Marine and bought the White Star Line in 1902.

The second of the 'Big Four' liners, *Cedric*, entered service on 11 February 1903. She was similar to *Celtic*[2] in design and similarly was noted for her ability to remain steady in the roughest weather.

Although Ismay was still chairman and managing director of the White Star Line, Morgan wanted him also to take over as president of IMM. Initially he refused but agreed, at least, to talk to Morgan about the proposition, and on 24 January 1904 he sailed for New York aboard the *Oceanic*[2].

On 21 February J. Bruce Ismay wrote to Charles Steele, one of J. P. Morgan's advisors, accepting the position as president of the IMM Company.

From the moment the agreement, which took the form of a memo, was signed, J. Bruce Ismay was in complete charge of everything that happened within IMM. Not only did he control everything but he would also have been kept informed, one way or another, of everything that was going on within the company, and there was a lot going on.

***Top right:* An official White Star card for both *Celtic*[2] (1901) and *Cedric*, exemplifying just how similar the two vessels were.**

***Centre right: Runic* (1899).**

***Below: Cedric*, the second of White Star's 'Big Four' liners, entered service in 1903.**

***Above: Cretic* leaving Gibraltar.**

***Left: Cretic* leaving Ponta Delgada.**

***Bottom left: Cretic* (1902). Originally built for the Leyland Line as the *Hanoverian*, she transferred to White Star in 1903.**

At the time Ismay took over as president of IMM his long-time associate James Pirrie was in serious financial trouble. Having started construction of the new *Baltic*[2] for White Star, Harland & Wolff found that it did not have enough money and needed to borrow from Morgan to complete the vessel.

In 1903 White Star took over the Dominion Line steamer *Commonwealth* and renamed her *Canopic*. The three-year-old, 13,000-ton vessel would remain with White Star until she was scrapped in 1925. Shortly after taking on *Canopic* the line also took over the nine-year-old, 8,249-ton *American*. This vessel was renamed *Cufic*[2], and she, too, would serve faithfully, for 20 years. Following this acquisition, the *European* was brought in and renamed *Tropic*[2]. The 8,230-ton vessel, which had been built in 1896, would remain with the White Star Line until 1923.

Baltic[2], the third of the 'Big Four' White Star liners, entered service in 1904. Like her sisters *Celtic*[2] and *Cedric* she was never intended to be particularly fast but was meant to provide a steady, comfortable passage for those aboard her. Because Ismay had

***Above: Cretic* in the Mersey.**

***Left: Canopic* (1900). Originally the Dominion Line's *Commonwealth*, she transferred to White Star in 1903.**

***Above right: Canopic* in the River Mersey.**

***Right: Canopic* at Palermo.**

wanted the new *Baltic*[2] to be the world's largest ship, her hull had been lengthened at quite a late stage in her construction.

In 1906 the first of Cunard's new, Government-subsidised super-liners was launched, a vessel destined to become almost as well known as the most famous of White Star's own super-liners. She was the *Lusitania*. It was the coming of these Cunard vessels that spurred White Star on, to construct even bigger and better liners of its own.

Early in 1907 it was decided that the fastest ships of the White Star Line, engaged on the North Atlantic routes, should sail from Southampton instead of Liverpool. There were several reasons for the decision but the most important was simply that the Hampshire port was closer to London.

Suevic, homeward bound from Australia, left Tenerife for Plymouth, where she was supposed to land some of her passengers, on 13 March 1907. She made good time, exceeding 13kt, until at midday on 17 March she was 138 miles from the Lizard light on England's southwest coast, heading towards this well-known danger area. At about 10.25 that evening the lookout reported breakers ahead of the ship. The chief engineer, who happened to be on deck, suddenly made out the Lizard light at the very moment the lookout raised the alarm. The engineer also saw breakers on the port side of the ship. The captain ordered the helm 'hard-a-port' but before the vessel could respond she crashed on the Maenheere Rocks, a quarter of a mile from Lizard Point, still at full speed. (Helm orders were a leftover from the days when ships were steered with a tiller and meant exactly the opposite to what they appear to mean. The helm order 'hard-a-port' actually meant 'put the rudder hard-a-starboard'.) The engines were put full astern to see if the ship might drag herself off but she was hard aground and refused to move. After about half an hour coastguards at Lizard Point noticed the frantic signals coming from *Suevic*, and the Lizard and Falmouth lifeboats went to the rescue.

WHITE STAR
LINE.
"CANOPIC," AT PALERMO

" END OF THE VOYAGE."
"Farewell to Liverpool" Liner

Far left: Baltic[2] in the River Mersey. One of White Star's 'Big Four' liners, she was the largest ship in the world when she entered service in 1904.

Bottom left: Baltic[2] leaving the landing stage at Liverpool.

Left: Baltic[2] seen at the landing stage at Liverpool.

Below: Baltic[2].

WRECK OF THE WHITE STAR LINER "SUEVIC" AT THE LIZARD, CORNWALL, MARCH 17TH 1907. No 7.

WHITE STAR LINE.

AUSTRALIAN SERVICE

VIA CAPETOWN.

S.S "SUEVIC"

19

Above: Suevic hard aground near the Lizard, Cornwall. The photograph is dated on the postcard 17 March 1907.

Left: White Star ship's stationery from *Suevic*, on which passengers would have recorded details of the vessel's grounding in letters to friends and relatives.

Below: Another photograph of *Suevic* aground on Sunday 17 March 1907.

Top right: In order to save the bigger part of *Suevic*, the bow, which was firmly stuck on the rocks, had to be cut off and abandoned, as seen here.

Right: The stern section of *Suevic* was taken to Southampton to have a new bow fitted. The extremely efficient cutting of the hull with dynamite is clearly shown.

White Star Liner "Suevic"
Wrecked at the Lizard on
Sunday March 17th 1907.
Photo by A.H. Hawke's

Southampton 1907
No 11.
PORTION OF THE "SUEVIC" SHOWING THE END WHICH WAS CUT WITH
PHOTO. TAKEN WHEN IN SOUTHAMPTON DOCKS, AFTER BEING TOWED

Right: Souvenir card commemorating the inauguration of White Star's regular service from Southampton in 1907.

Above right: Adriatic[2], which launched the White Star Line's regular transatlantic service between Southampton and New York.

Far right: Official White Star card showing *Adriatic*[2].

Nine days later *Suevic* was still firmly aground. It was decided that there were only two options open: either the vessel would have to be abandoned, or the stern section would have to be cut from the grounded bow and salvaged separately. White Star opted for the second alternative. The operation was duly completed and *Suevic's* truncated stern section was taken to Southampton to have a new bow fitted. The new forward hull section was built at Harland & Wolff's. Both it and the original ship had been so accurately constructed that no problems at all were encountered when the two halves were joined.

On the afternoon of 8 January 1908 *Suevic* left drydock, moved to a coaling berth and began to take on fuel ready for her short trip to Liverpool, which began just two days later. All the effort involved in salvaging the *Suevic* proved well worth while for she served the line well until she was sold off in 1928.

A new era for the line began in May 1907 when *Celtic*^{2} took the first, experimental, voyage from Southampton to New York. A month later a regular service began. The new Southampton to New York run would be maintained by the *Adriatic*^{2}, *Oceanic*^{2}, *Teutonic* and the *Majestic*^{1}. The trendsetting *Celtic*^{2} returned to the old established Liverpool route.

Adriatic^2, the last of the 'Big Four', entered service in 1907. She was even larger than the *Baltic*^{2}, at 24,540 tons, and had much more powerful engines. She was also the first ship to have Turkish baths and a swimming pool aboard. The 'Big Four' was one of the most successful series of liners ever built and the liners worked on the service to America almost constantly from 1907 to 1928.

In response to Cunard's new super-liners, Ismay and Pirrie decided to build something even better – in fact, three somethings. Not only would they be more opulent than either the *Lusitania* or the *Mauritania*, the new liners were to be half as large again as the Cunard flagships. They were planned to be the largest man-made moving objects on earth. With two reciprocating engines, the new liners were expected to return a speed of 21kt.

The nominal chief designer at Harland & Wolff was the Honourable Alexander Carlisle, Pirrie's brother-in-law. Originally, Carlisle wanted 64 lifeboats but this was considered extravagant and the numbers were reduced first to 48, then to 32 and finally to 16.

Left: Adriatic[2] **passing the Needles off the Isle of Wight.**

***Below:* *Adriatic*[2] (1907), at Prince's Landing Stage, Liverpool, in about 1907. She was the last of White Star's 'Big Four' liners.**

***Right:* Postcard of *Megantic* leaving Liverpool.**

There needed to be only one complete set of drawings as the ships were to be identical and would be built from the same plan. As the new vessels became available, they were intended to replace the 'Big Four' on the Southampton service.

The keel of the first of the new super-liners, *Olympic*, was laid on 16 December 1908. The main part of the hull was subdivided into 16 separate compartments by 15 transverse bulkheads. The ships were designed to remain afloat with any four forward compartments flooded. As planned, the new '*Olympic*' class ships were to be 882ft 6in long and 92ft 6in wide. Weighing 45,324 gross register tons but displacing (actual all-up-weight) about 66,000 tons, they would be, by a comfortable margin, the largest vessels in the world.

Still unconvinced by the novel technology of the turbine engines, White Star instructed Harland & Wolff, which had a couple of new IMM vessels under construction, to fit one of them, the new *Megantic*, with traditional reciprocating engines, and the other, *Laurentic*[1], with a combination of turbine and reciprocating. There turned out to be little difference in the overall top speed of the two vessels but there was a marked increase in fuel economy with the turbine-powered vessel. It was only then decided that the new super-liners should have the combination of power plants that had performed so economically in the *Laurentic*[1].

Early in 1909 a White Star liner was involved in another accident. On 10 January the 5,118-ton Lloyd Italiano vessel *Florida* sailed from Naples. *Republic*[2] set out from New York on

Left: **Card from *Laurentic*[1] (1908).**

***Below: Laurentic*[1] was built for the Liverpool to Canada service. She had an experimental combination of turbine and reciprocating engines.**

the return leg of a journey from Genoa on 22 January. On the following day, in thick fog, she was rammed by the inbound *Florida*. A huge hole was torn in *Republic's* side just aft of her funnel and 30ft of *Florida's* bow was crushed like a concertina.

Aboard *Republic*[2] three people died as a direct result of the collision. Working under almost impossible conditions and holding his equipment together with his bare hands, wireless operator Jack

White Star Line. R. M. S. "Republic". Twin Screw.
15400 Tons.

WHITE STAR LINE
"REPUBLIC" AT NAPLES
Charles Dixon

Left: Republic[2] (1903), which sank off Martha's Vineyard following a collision with the *Florida* in 1909.

Below left: Republic[2] at Naples.

R.M.S. "Megantic."
WHITE STAR-DOMINION LINE.
TWIN-SCREW R.M.S. "MEGANTIC," 14,878 TONS, ARRIVING MONTREAL.

Top: Republic[2] at Prince's Landing Stage, Liverpool.

Above: Megantic (1908). Sister ship to *Laurentic*, she was built with only traditional reciprocating engines.

Left: Megantic arriving at Montreal.

Left: **Some of the crew of the tender *Traffic*[2] (1911), which was built to carry passengers to and from the new 'Olympic' class ships at Cherbourg because the liners were too big to get into the harbour.**

Below left: **Dignitaries from International Mercantile Marine watch from the ferry as *Olympic* (out of view) leaves the builders in May 1911.**

Binns managed to summon *Baltic*[2] to the ships' assistance. She arrived at about 7.30pm, more than 12 hours after the collision, and in a four-hour operation took aboard all of *Republic*'s passengers. Shortly before midnight she began to evacuate the passengers aboard *Florida*, taking no less than 1,650 from that vessel.

Shortly after 8.30pm on 24 January *Republic*[2] disappeared beneath the waves. With the loss of the *Republic*, the White Star Line possessed the unfortunate record of owning the largest ship to have foundered at sea. That record would stand for just three years before the same company rewrote it.

On 31 March 1909 the keel of the second '*Olympic*' class vessel was laid. At the time construction began, this ship, *Titanic*, was intended to be identical to *Olympic*, but minor changes would be made after the maiden voyage of the first of the class, making *Titanic* about a thousand tons heavier than her sister.

The ex-Dominion Line ships *Albany* and *Alberta* entered service with White Star in 1909, renamed *Laurentic*[1] and *Megantic*. *Laurentic* would win lasting notoriety in 1917 when she struck a mine and sank off the Irish coast with a cargo of gold bullion aboard.

Olympic was launched on 20 October 1910. Only the finest craftsmen were employed in fitting out the first class passenger accommodation, which was of a style and standard that would not have disgraced a first class hotel of the time. Second and third class cabins and public rooms were also well above the standards of other lines.

In preparation for the new '*Olympic*' class liners, which would be far too large to enter the port of Cherbourg, the line had commissioned two new tenders to carry passengers out to the leviathans. These vessels, which came into service in 1911, were the 1,273-ton *Nomadic* and the 675-ton *Traffic*. Both of these small vessels would have long and chequered careers.

Olympic, after only two days of fairly exhaustive trials, was ready to be handed over to her new owners by Harland & Wolff on 31 May 1911. To gain extra publicity, the second behemoth would be launched on the same day that the handing over ceremony took place. After *Titanic*'s launch *Olympic* left for Liverpool, with Morgan, Ismay, his daughter and the other dignitaries on board. At Liverpool she was thrown open to the public. After a day in Liverpool *Olympic* left for Southampton to prepare for her maiden voyage, arriving there in the early hours of 3 June.

Under the command of Captain Edward John Smith, she sailed on 14 June 1911 for New York, accompanied by Joseph Bruce Ismay and his wife. Ismay noted one or two minor items that he thought could be improved upon aboard the second of the new '*Olympics*', such as extra cabins on B deck.

On 20 September an incident occurred that, in the authors' opinion, marked the beginning of the end for the White Star Line.

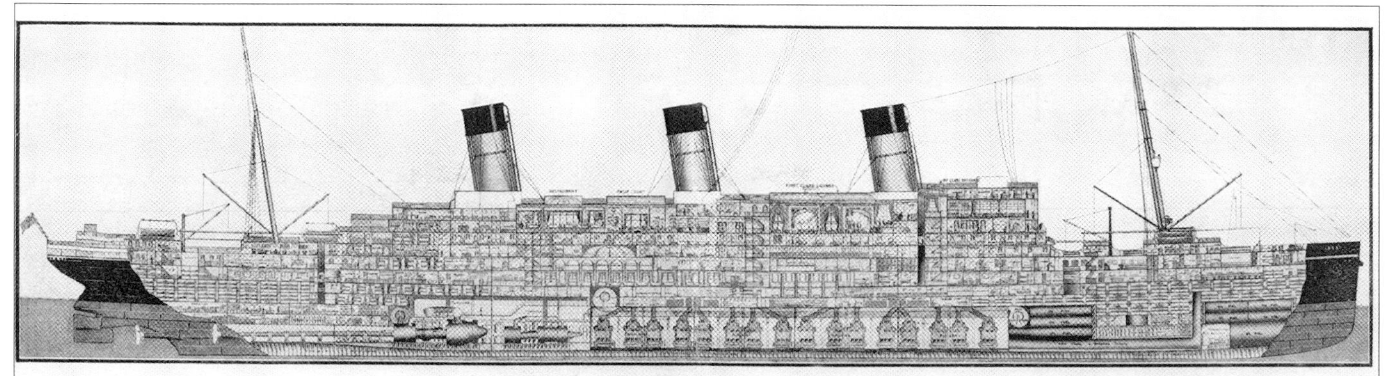

THE "MAJESTIC" (56,551 TONS) SHOWN IN SECTION.
Length 954·6 feet, breadth 100·6 feet, depth (from keel to boat deck) 102 feet. Quadruple screws. Speed 24 knots.

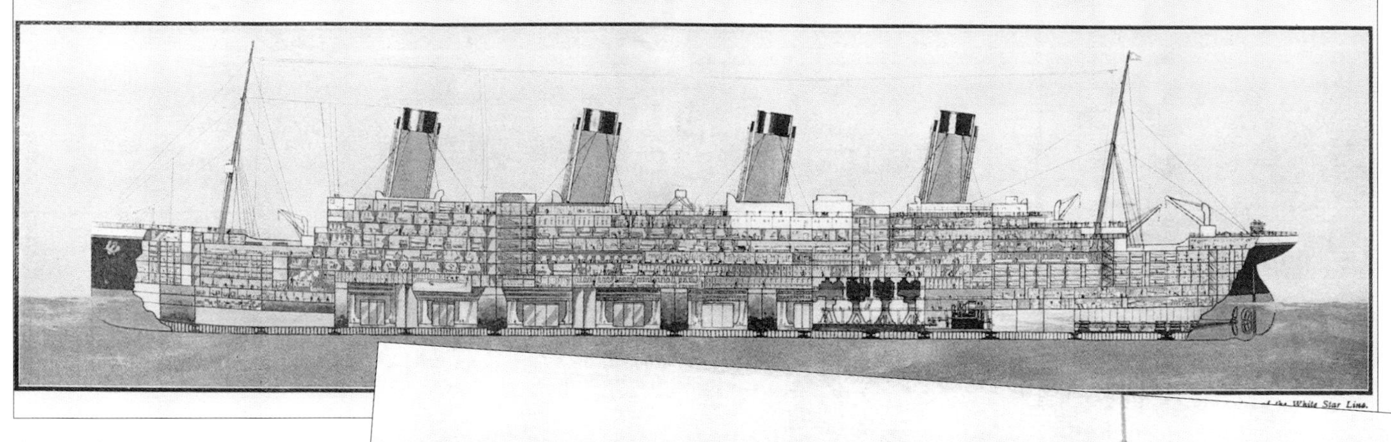

***Above:* Sectional views showing the layout of *Majestic*[2] (1914) and *Olympic* (1911). When built, *Majestic* (the ex-German liner Bismarck) was the largest ship in the world.**

***Right: Olympic* in 1911.**

As *Olympic*, with Captain E. J. Smith and the harbour pilot George William Bowyer on the bridge, was leaving Southampton Water at the start of her fifth westbound Atlantic crossing she was rammed in the starboard quarter by the Royal Navy's armoured cruiser HMS *Hawke* and suffered such serious damage that she had to return to the builders for a full two months of repairs.

In the meantime, the keel of the third '*Olympic*' class vessel, *Britannic*[2], was laid, as far as it is known, on 30 November 1911. Even the original name for this third '*Olympic*' is not certain, but it is believed to have been *Gigantic*.

Olympic left New York on 21 February 1912 following her repairs and outward bound trip to New York, heading for Southampton. Three days out, while about 750 miles east of Newfoundland, she ran over what is understood to have been a submerged wreck and broke a blade off her port

Right: Olympic is seen arriving at Liverpool on 1 June 1911 before proceeding to Southampton to prepare for her maiden voyage to New York.

Below: Olympic's first commander, Captain Edward John Smith, is seen with his family in 1910. E. J. Smith, Commodore of the White Star Line, was the most highly paid captain of the time.

WHITE STAR LINE

TWIN SCREW STEAMER "OCEANIC"

2ND CLASS.

DECEMBER 19TH 1911

LUNCHEON.

Printaniere Soup

Weakfish, Meuniere

Rabbit Pie, Anglaise
Ox Tail a la Jardiniere
Baked Jacket & Mashed Potatoes

COLD

Roast Beef
Ox Tongue | York Ham
Bologna Sausage

Potato Salad

Roll Jam Pudding | Pumpkin Pie

Cheese | Biscuits | Coffee

Left: **Second class luncheon menu from *Oceanic*[2] in 1911. The selection of cold meats is some indication of what was eaten for dinner in first class the evening before.**

Left: **On 20 September 1911, while she was just to the north of Cowes on the Isle of Wight, *Olympic* was rammed in the starboard quarter by HMS *Hawke*, as shown by this contemporary picture. Both vessels were severely damaged in the collision.**

Top: **Following the *Hawke* incident, *Olympic's* starboard propeller and shaft had to be replaced with similar parts intended for her younger sister, *Titanic*, which was still under construction at Belfast.**

White Star Liner "Olympic."
Launched 20th October, 1910.
45,000 Tons ; Speed, 21 knots.
Length, 883 ft. ;
Breadth, 93 ft. : Depth, 97 ft.

R.M.S "TITANIC"
LEAVING SOUTHAMPTON
APRIL 10TH 1912

***Left: Olympic* at sea sometime before late April 1912.**

***Bottom left: Titanic* (1912), the second *'Olympic'* class ship, leaving Southampton at the start of her maiden, and only, voyage.**

***Below: Titanic* moving out of Southampton Water.**

***Below right:* Cherbourg in 1912.**

main propeller. Despite the loss of the propeller blade, and consequently the use of the port main engine, *Olympic* arrived at Southampton on 28 February. She left Southampton for Belfast the following day, making for the only drydock in the world big enough to take her, to have a new propeller blade fitted. What should have been a one-day job took a full week to complete.

On All Fools' Day 1912 fire broke out in No 10 bunker aboard the brand-new *Titanic*, which was awaiting her acceptance trials at Belfast. At 6 o'clock in the morning of the next day, the second of the White Star Line's new leviathans began her 'trials', which lasted a short working day, under the command of Captain E. J. Smith. After the 'trials' *Titanic* headed directly for Southampton, without being opened to the public at Liverpool as her sister had been. Public inspection of the ship was also denied at the Hampshire port.

Titanic reached Southampton at a few minutes after midnight, early in the morning of Thursday 4 April 1912. The ship was due to sail on her maiden voyage on the 10th and had to be coaled and provisioned. There were still workmen aboard finishing various jobs, and the bunker fire still had not been put out.

Because of a major coal strike then in progress, harbours around Britain were crowded with ships that could not get enough coal to fill their bunkers. To collect enough coal for *Titanic* to reach New York the bunkers of five other IMM ships laid up in Southampton were stripped bare. In an act of almost unimaginable stupidity, Captain E. J. Smith allowed tons of coal to be poured into *Titanic*'s already burning bunker No 10.

J. Bruce Ismay and Thomas Andrews, Pirrie's nephew and Managing Director at Harland & Wolff, with an eight-man group of skilled workers representing the builders, were to sail with the ship.

On 10 April the *Titanic* sailed from Southampton on her maiden voyage to New York, via Cherbourg and Queenstown. On the first leg of the voyage the lookouts discovered that they had no binoculars supplied, which was unusual. Other than that, the initial part of the crossing went relatively smoothly, but it was not to last.

In the time that she had been at sea the *Titanic* had received many warnings from other vessels of ice in her path. Then, at 11.40pm on Sunday 14 April, the lookouts reported ice ahead of the ship. Mr Murdoch, the First Officer, ordered the helm hard-a-starboard and the engines full astern, but it was too late. *Titanic* struck the iceberg a glancing blow on her starboard side. The impact was apparently hardly noticed by most aboard but the ship was mortally wounded. The liner could remain afloat with any four forward compartments flooded, but not with all five.

Captain Smith ordered the boats to be swung out and loaded with women and children. Unfortunately, the ship had only enough lifeboats to accommodate about half of those aboard her. Red, white and blue distress rockets were also sent up in the hope of

***Above:* Is this the iceberg that sank the *Titanic*? This photograph was formerly the property of Charles Victor Groves, Third Officer of the *Californian*, and was taken on the morning of 15 April 1912 as the *Californian* helped to rescue survivors from the *Titanic*.**

***Right: Titanic's* bandmaster, Wallace Hartley, with his music tutor, Pickles Riley. Hartley was to perish with the ship.**

attracting the attention of another steamer which could be seen about five miles away, without result.

The wireless operators managed to contact the Cunard liner *Carpathia*, almost 60 miles away. The Cunarder started toward *Titanic* without delay and Captain Rostron worked his ship up to 17½kt as he raced to the rescue, 3½kt faster than she had ever been intended to travel. It would take *Carpathia* about four hours to reach the position of the *Titanic*, 41°46'N. 50°14'W, while it would take the White Star giant only 2½ hours to sink.

Shortly after 2am on 15 April *Titanic* buried her bows beneath the cold, black waters of the North Atlantic. By 2.15 the stern of the great ship was sticking vertically up out of the water, like a giant tombstone. At 2.20am the waters of the Atlantic Ocean closed over what has since been described as the 'Greatest of the Works of Man'.

Carpathia arrived at the scene of the disaster at about 4 o'clock in the morning and began to pick up the people from the lifeboats in the area. Four and a half hours later Captain Rostron had 705 survivors from *Titanic* aboard his ship. Among them was J. Bruce Ismay. As *Carpathia* was collecting the last of the survivors another ship came up to join them, the Leyland Line's *Californian*.

At the time *Titanic* had sent out her first wireless distress signals the *Californian* was lying, stopped by the ice, 19½ miles away, to the north, much too far away for the stricken liner's rockets and Morse lamp to have been seen.

Once the survivors reached America an official Government inquiry into the disaster was begun, at which selected witnesses were called to give evidence. Those members of the liner's crew not required by the inquiry were, for most of their stay in America, held incommunicado aboard the Red Star Line's *Lapland*.

The American inquiry could be best described in the words of *Titanic's* senior surviving officer Charles Herbert Lightoller – 'A farce'. The British inquiry, held a little later, was no better, being a rather obvious and relatively successful cover-up.

As a consequence of the *Titanic* disaster, work on *Britannic*[2] was suspended while the vessel was redesigned so as to be immune to the sort of damage that had sunk her sister at the cost of so many lives. One result of the alterations was the provision of eight pairs of large, and unsightly, gantry davits, each capable of handling six 34ft lifeboats. Forty-eight such boats could support all 3,522 people that the ship was designed to carry.

Before *Olympic* could be allowed to sail again, on Ismay's specific direction, enough lifeboats would also have to be provided on her for every person aboard. On 11 August 1912 White Star announced that it was withdrawing *Olympic* from service in November for a complete overhaul. The decision was influenced, no doubt, by the understandable reluctance of a travelling public to entrust its lives to a type of vessel, described by the press earlier as 'practically unsinkable', that had so spectacularly demonstrated just how 'unsinkable' it was.

Above: The old town gateway at Southampton in 1912. By far the majority of the sailors lost with the *Titanic* came from Southampton.

Left: Extra collapsible lifeboats were put aboard *Olympic* following the *Titanic* disaster.

Below: A view of *Titanic* lifeboats and wreckage being shipped to Southampton on the *Olympic*.

ARMS OF LIVERPOOL
Liverpool. Landing Stage.
"Silverette"

PIER PIERROTS
LANDING STAGE, LIVERPOOL.

Right: **Liverpool colliers are seen taking a break from coaling a ship in about 1900.**

Left and below: **Three late Edwardian views of the Liverpool landing stage.**

Bottom right: **White Star passengers aboard the Liverpool tender *Magnetic*.**

Left: Colliers working aboard White Star's *Cedric*.

Bottom: Romanic (1899) at Liverpool. Originally the Dominion Line's *New England*, she was transferred to White Star in 1903.

Below: White Star passengers aboard the tender *Gallic*.

Above: Prince's Landing Stage, Liverpool.

Left: Some of the workers from Harland & Wolff who built the ships for White Star.

HAZEL KIRKE

CANADA DOCK, LIVERPOOL

Right: The cover of the List of Cabin Passengers aboard *Cretic* in the early years of the 20th century.

LIST OF CABIN PASSENGERS

S. S "CRETIC"

Twin Screw - 13,518 Tons

WHITE STAR LINE

NEW YORK – LIVERPOOL

Left: The notorious reception centre at Ellis Island was the first port of call at New York for all transatlantic immigrant ships.

Bottom left: Liverpool docks c1905 with four White Star liners tied up: *Ceramic* (bottom left), *Celtic*[2] (top left), *Majestic*[1] (bottom right) and *Republic*[2] (top right).

Right: An 'Olympic'-type anchor, made at Noah Hingley's foundry at Netherton, Birmingham, on its way to Belfast.

Below: The Seaman's Orphanage in Liverpool in about 1905. Frederick Fleet, the senior lookout on duty aboard RMS *Titanic* at 11.40pm on 14 April 1912, was raised here.

Below: **The house flags, funnel colours and signal flags used by the major North Atlantic shipping companies in 1900.**

NE.
D
ALSO NO
F
G
AMERICAN LINE.
H
HAMBURG LINE.
J
EXPRESS SERVICE
REGULAR SERVICE HAS BLACK
FUNNELS
FRENCH LINE.
K
L
ANCHOR LINE.
M
NETHERLANDS LINE.
N.A.S.M.
NATIONAL LINE.
N

Top: Liverpool landing stage in about 1906/7.

Above: Liverpool landing stage c1910.

Left: Arabic[2] (1903). She was built as *Minnewaska* for the Atlantic Transport Line but transferred to White Star on completion.

THE LONG SLIDE TO OBLIVION

Olympic returned to Harland & Wolff in late 1912 to have her bulkheads raised and an entire inner skin fitted to her hull. As originally designed, like *Titanic* she could continue to float with any two of her major compartments flooded, but after the work was completed she was able to remain afloat with six such compartments open to the sea. By the time the alterations to her safety features were complete, at a cost of £250,000 in early 1913, she was probably the safest ship in the world.

The number of lifeboats aboard was increased from the original, and wholly inadequate, 20 to 68, four more than Alexander Carlisle had wanted to put on the ship when he first designed her lifeboat layout. In all, the improvements to *Olympic* took five months to complete.

As a direct result of the loss of the *Titanic*, in early 1913 the United States Government started the North Atlantic Ice Patrol to keep a check on icebergs. The patrol continues to the present day, and on every 15 April lays a wreath on the sea at 41°46'N. 50°14'W.

While on a trip to Europe and Egypt, J. P. Morgan, who had not been a well man for some while, steadily began to decline. While in Rome the decline continued until he lapsed into a coma, regaining consciousness only fitfully. He died in his sleep on the night of 31 March 1913.

That same year the 18,481-ton *Ceramic* entered service with White Star on the Australian route. At the time she was the largest vessel to frequent antipodean shores.

Olympic completed her refit and left Harland & Wolff's yard on 22 March 1913. For the next year and a half she plied back and forth between Southampton and New York without any problems and so began to lay the ghost of her departed sister, and gain in popularity.

On 30 June 1913 J. Bruce Ismay retired from the presidency of IMM and the White Star Line. With him went the name of his father's old company, Ismay, Imrie & Co, which became his exclusive property. On Ismay's retirement, Harold Sanderson took over as president of IMM.

The third and last of the '*Olympic*' class vessels, *Britannic*[2], was launched on 26 February 1914. Work on the new liner could progress only very slowly because of difficulties in obtaining materials. Although Harland & Wolff had no new vessels on order by the Admiralty, many other yards did, and with the threat of war looming these other yards were getting priority. *Britannic* would never be completed as a liner.

Left: **'Sailor Bill' c1930. After long and faithful service to the White Star Line some seamen, typified by 'Sailor Bill', were retired to serve on tenders in the Mersey.**

Throughout the summer of 1914 tension grew between the countries of Europe. The coming of war had long been foreseen and international organisations had done their best to defuse the situation. Unfortunately, many of the more influential members of those organisations had been aboard the *Titanic*, going to a special peace rally in New York.

In June 1914 the Austrian Archduke Franz Ferdinand and his wife were murdered by Serbian nationalists as they visited the Bosnian town of Sarajevo. A month later, on 28 July, Austria declared war on Serbia. The great European powers – Germany, France, Britain and Russia – mobilised for war. Russia sided with Serbia, while Germany backed her old ally Austria. Germany was ready first and immediately launched an assault on France, through Belgium. Britain had a treaty with Belgium and so, on 4 August, declared war on Germany. The Great War had begun.

Right: Donkeys on the sands at Morecambe in 1914, with *Majestic*[1] in the background awaiting scrapping.

Below: Majestic[1] is seen completing her final voyage, to Morecambe and the breaker's.

Right: Olympic in the floating dock at Southampton. The photograph is believed to date from the late 1920s.

Bottom right: Ceramic (1913) berthing at Liverpool. The picture is believed to date from the 1920s.

Below: Olympic in the 1920s, with the upper deck crowded with lifeboats.

Landing Stage Liverpool.

WHITE STAR
LINE.
"CERAMIC" AT SEA

WHITE STAR LINE R.M.S. "BRITANNIC" 50,000 TONS–ON THE STOCKS
Models of WHITE STAR Steamers "BRITANNIC" 5,000 tons, built in 1874, and "BRITANNIC," 50,000 tons, built in 1914.

***Above left:* *Ceramic*.**

***Left:* *Ceramic* at sea.**

***Below:* The launch of *Britannic*[2] (1914). The third and last of the *'Olympic'* class liners, *Britannic* never sailed in White Star livery nor carried a fare-paying passenger.**

***Top:* *Britannic*[2] (1914) on the stocks at Belfast.**

***Above:* The builder's models of *Britannic*[1] and *Britannic*[2], showing the difference in size between the two vessels, and how the second ship was originally intended to look in life, rather than her eventual appearance.**

Olympic left Southampton for New York on 29 July 1914, just six days before hostilities between Britain and Germany broke out. On hearing of the declaration of war, Captain Haddock ordered wireless silence and *Olympic* was blacked out. She was escorted into New York by the Royal Navy's cruiser HMS *Essex*. During the four-day layover in New York the crew practised the blackout and painted the superstructure of the ship dull grey. On Saturday 8 August 1914, without any passengers, cargo or mail aboard, *Olympic* suddenly left New York on the return leg of her voyage, again escorted by the *Essex*. She left the *Essex* behind at Sable Island and crossed the Atlantic alone. As she approached the Irish coast she was met by another cruiser, HMS *Drake*, which escorted her into Liverpool on the 15th.

Because of the difficulties in finding a safe berth for *Olympic*, and the fact that she presented a prime target for the enemy, it was decided to lay her up. On 21 October she left New York on the return leg of a transatlantic voyage, heading first for the Clyde and then Belfast where she would be safe. She had almost completed the passage when, on the morning of 27 October, the liner went to the rescue of the brand-new battleship, HMS *Audacious*, which had struck a mine in the Irish Sea and was sinking. *Olympic* lowered her own boats to take off some of the crew of the crippled warship, and in less than two hours all but 250 of her people had been rescued and her boats recovered. The remainder of the battleship's crew were eventually taken on board *Olympic* and the cruiser HMS *Liverpool*. *Olympic* arrived at Belfast on 2 November, having been detained by the Royal Navy for a week after the sinking of the *Audacious*. Now she was to undergo a 10-month refit in preparation for war service as a troopship.

Earlier in 1914, on 9 July, *Justicia* had been launched by Harland & Wolff as the *Statendam* for the Holland-America Line. She was 740ft 6in long, 86ft 5in wide and weighed 32,232 gross tons. The British Admiralty took her over and completed her to its own specifications before handing her to White Star.

Inevitably, the war would bring losses to all major shipowners, including White Star. On 8 September 1914 the *Oceanic*[2] ran aground on the Shaalds of Foula. The crew were taken off and most of the armaments were removed before the *Oceanic* was abandoned to her fate. For nine years the vessel remained, pounded by the waves, before she was finally destroyed in a great storm.

Other wartime replacements saw the 14-year-old *Vaderland* being transferred to White Star from another line within the IMM Group, Red Star, in 1914. The 12,017-ton vessel was renamed *Southland*.

Cevic was requisitioned by the British Government in 1915 and converted into a dummy battlecruiser, the '*Queen Mary*'. The presence of what was believed to be the battlecruiser *Queen Mary*

Below: **Liverpool pierhead c1913.**

Left: **White Star seamen wearing their lifejackets on a Liverpool landing stage in 1916.**

Below: **The cover of a White Star passenger's brochure from the second decade of the 20th century.**

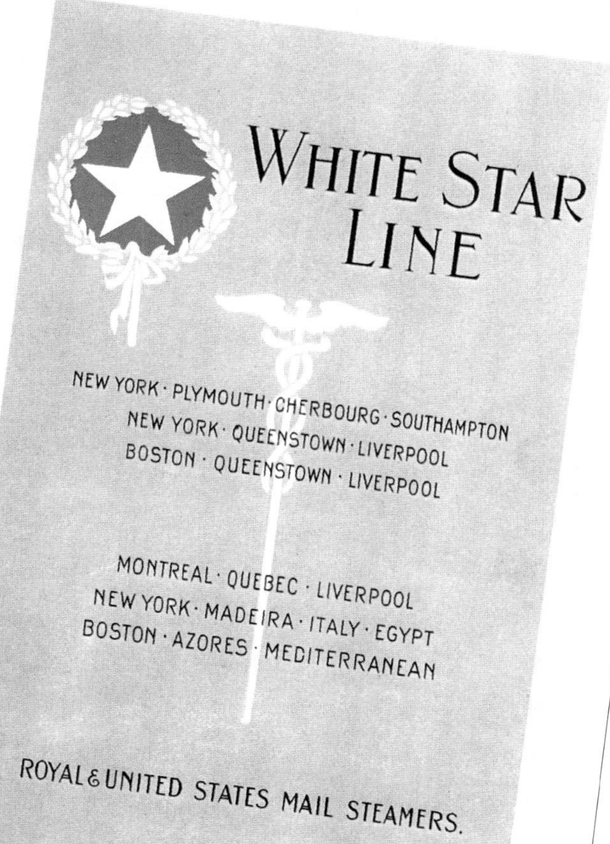

off New York was the principal reason for the surrender, and subsequent internment, of the German liner *Kronprinz Wilhelm*.

WHITE STAR
LINE
NEW YORK · PLYMOUTH · CHERBOURG · SOUTHAMPTON
NEW YORK · QUEENSTOWN · LIVERPOOL
BOSTON · QUEENSTOWN · LIVERPOOL
MONTREAL · QUEBEC · LIVERPOOL
NEW YORK · MADEIRA · ITALY · EGYPT
BOSTON · AZORES · MEDITERRANEAN
ROYAL & UNITED STATES MAIL STEAMERS.

In 1910, 1911, 1914 and 1915 the White Star Line had chartered the 11,905-ton *Zeeland* from Red Star. During the war years the ship's name was to be changed to *Northland*.

While serving as a troopship in the Salonika campaign, on 15 September 1915 *Southland* (ex-*Vaderland*) was torpedoed in the Aegean Sea, but managed to limp into port for repairs.

In 1915 the Admiralty bought the *Teutonic* outright from White Star, supposedly for use as a troopship, but she was returned to the line in 1918. *Cufic*[2] was pressed into service as an armed merchant cruiser in the same year, but was later found not to be ideal for that purpose and was converted for use as a troopship.

On her way to New York from Liverpool on 19 August 1915, *Arabic*[2], under the command of Lieutenant Will Finch RNR, was off the Old Head of Kinsale, at the southern tip of Ireland, when she was torpedoed by *U24*. Although at that time German submarines were under orders not to torpedo passenger ships without warning, Lieutenant Commander Schneider, believing that *Arabic* was trying to ram his boat, felt justified in ignoring those orders. *Arabic* sank in just 11 minutes, taking 44 of the 253 crew and 181 passengers with her.

At 10 o'clock on the morning of 24 September 1915 the *Olympic* left Liverpool on her first voyage as a troopship, bound for Mudros with 6,000 troops aboard. As the war went on she would switch from carrying troops to the Dardanelles theatre to bringing them from Canada and then America to England, earning a nickname that remained with her for the rest of her long working life, 'Old Reliable'.

Britannic[2], the third and last of the '*Olympic*' class ships built for the White Star Line was taken over by the Admiralty on 13 November 1915 for use as a hospital ship, and was fitted out as such. Her construction had been held up by the *Titanic* disaster and the ensuing inquiry, and again by a shortage of available materials once the war began. Intended to be the last, and best, of her class, she was slightly larger than her two more famous sisters, 5ft longer and almost 2,000 tons heavier. She arrived in the Mersey on 12 December 1915 and was handed over to the Admiralty, which commissioned her as His Majesty's Hospital Ship *Britannic*. Command was given to Captain Charles A. Bartlett, who had been with White Star for 21 years. *Olympic* was still at Liverpool when *Britannic* arrived. *Britannic* left on 23 December and *Olympic* 12 days later, on 4 January 1916, both bound for the eastern Aegean.

At the beginning of the war the *Baltic*[2] and *Adriatic*[2] had continued to operate between Liverpool and New York, but as the war progressed they were pressed into service as troopships. The *Adriatic* acquired the nickname 'Queen of the Munitions Fleet'. It was the *Baltic* that brought the very first American troops to England when the United States somewhat belatedly declared war on Germany in 1917. She carried a plaque commemorating the event for the rest of her working life.

Olympic had been created for use on the North Atlantic and her coal bunker capacity had been limited to just enough to make such voyages comfortably. In March 1916 the Canadian Government chartered her to ferry troops from Halifax to Britain, a task for which she was tailor-made. From the fourth week in March 1916 until the beginning of 1917 *Olympic* sailed across the Atlantic between Liverpool and Halifax no fewer than 20 times carrying Canadian troops, without any sort of escort. In that time more than 50,000 troops were carried.

At about 4pm on 8 May 1916 *Cymric*, on her way to Liverpool from New York, was hit by three torpedoes fired from *U20*. The commander Walter Schwieger had, a year and a day earlier, sunk the Cunard liner *Lusitania*, which sank in 16 minutes after being hit by only one torpedo. *Cymric* remained afloat for almost a full day following the attack.

During the summer of 1916 heavy fighting flared up in Egypt and Palestine. *Britannic*[2] was again used by the British Government as a hospital ship. She sailed for Mudros to evacuate wounded on 23 September 1916.

Contrary to the rules of war, *Britannic*[2], as a hospital ship, did not transport only sick or wounded troops but also completely fit soldiers of the Royal Army Medical Corps. These soldiers were not aboard to tend the wounded but were merely being taken out to, or returning from, the areas where the war was being fought. This meant, of course, that *Britannic* was serving as a troopship and was therefore a legitimate target for the enemy.

On the morning of Tuesday 21 November 1916, while actually serving as a hospital ship, although luckily devoid of patients at the time, the *Britannic*[2] struck a mine in the Aegean Sea. She sank with the loss of 21 lives, most of which were victims of the vessel's own propellers, which were turning even as the lifeboats were lowered.

The losses of ex-White Star ships continued throughout the war. *Georgic*[1], which had joined the White Star fleet in 1895, was sunk by the German surface raider *Moewe* on 10 December 1916 while heading for Brest and Liverpool from Pennsylvania. One member of the crew was killed before the rest were taken off and the ship sunk by torpedo.

The 8,825-ton ex-Leyland Line's *Victorian*, which had been with White Star since 1903, lately as a cargo ship named *Russian*, was torpedoed while in the Mediterranean on 14 December 1916.

The 15,000-ton *Laurentic*[1], under the command of Captain Reginald A. Norton, sailed from Liverpool for Halifax with £5 million in gold aboard. On 25 January, off Malin Head, on the northwest coast of Ireland, she struck two mines and sank. The crew of 722 officers and men all managed to get into 15 lifeboats before the ship foundered, but eight of the boats never reached safety and 354 lives were lost.

The *Afric* was torpedoed, five miles south-southwest of the Eddystone lighthouse in the English Channel, while returning from Australia, on 12 February 1917. Five crewmen were killed by the explosion and a further 17 were drowned as they tried to abandon ship.

The *Southland*, ex-*Vaderland*, was sunk by the *U70* on 4 June 1917 with the loss of four lives. At the time of the sinking, the ship was about 140 miles northwest of Tory Point, Northern Ireland.

The 20-year-old, 8,273-ton *Delphic*[1], which had joined White Star in 1897, was torpedoed and sunk 135 miles southwest of Bishop Rock in the Scilly Isles, while on her way from Cardiff to Montevideo. Five lives were lost when the ship foundered with her cargo of coal on 16 August 1917.

In the last year of the war the ex-White Star ships continued to contribute to the war effort. On 11 January 1918 *Olympic* left New York with her first complement of American troops. During the war *Adriatic*[2], *Baltic*[2], *Cedric*, and *Celtic*[2] had not only served as troopships but also as auxiliary tankers carrying fuel for Royal Naval ships. The ships could each carry between 2,500 and 3,500 tons of fuel oil and between them brought in no less than 88,000 tons between August 1917 and the end of the war.

Soon after leaving Liverpool on 31 March 1918, the *Celtic*[2] was torpedoed by a German submarine. The torpedo killed six people and damaged the ship so badly that she had to be beached to prevent her from sinking. *Celtic* was eventually refloated and taken to Belfast for repairs.

On 12 May 1918, on her 22nd voyage as a troopship and with a full complement of American troops aboard, *Olympic*, while being escorted by four American destroyers through the hazardous waters of the English Channel, was attacked by the German submarine *U103*. *Olympic* not only managed to avoid the German torpedo but turned on her attacker so rapidly that she managed to ram the submarine and sink it.

Justicia left Liverpool on 18 July 1918. Shortly after 2pm the following day a torpedo from the *UB64* struck her port side, flooding the engine room and another compartment. However, the watertight bulkheads held, so the crew set about doing what they could to save the vessel. *Justicia* was taken in tow, but about 2½ hours after the first attack two more torpedoes were fired at her. One torpedo missed and the other was destroyed with gunfire from *Justicia's* crew. At about 8pm a fourth torpedo was fired at the troopship, but was again diverted by gunfire from the crew. At 4.30am the following morning another torpedo just missed the White Star vessel's bow; then at 9.30am *U54* fired a salvo of torpedoes at *Justicia's* port side, one struck No 3 hold and another No 5. *Justicia* sank stern first at 12.40pm on 20 July 1918.

While still 200 miles from the English coast, and with almost 3,000 American troops aboard, the *Persic* was torpedoed on 12 September 1918, and had to be beached. No lives were lost. Just under two months later, on 11 November 1918, the Great War came to its inconclusive end.

At the end of hostilities, vessels ordered by the Shipping Controller and just being completed came on the market. White

Above: Zealandic **(1911) at Liverpool c1912.**

Right: Zealandic **passengers celebrating shortly before the vessel departs Liverpool in 1927.**

Star promptly bought *War Priam*, an 8,000-ton cargo ship, in an effort to make good some of the losses its fleet of freighters had suffered. The company took over the vessel on 13 March 1919 and renamed the ship *Bardic*. She sailed on her maiden voyage for the line on the 18th.

On completion of her war work, lately transporting American servicemen back to their own country, *Olympic* returned to her Belfast builders for a complete refit. She arrived there on 12 August, having given extraordinary service for she had run almost nonstop for four years. This refit was something of a landmark in the history of North Atlantic passenger liner history as *Olympic* had her coal-fired system converted to oil, making her the first large Atlantic liner to be oil-fired.

Towards the end of 1918 the *Vedic* joined the White Star fleet. She was intended to be a one-class ship. There was no first and second class accommodation aboard, just third. But before she could begin to operate as such, she was employed in repatriating British troops.

At the war's end much of the German merchant fleet had been taken over by the Shipping Controller as 'War Reparations' and amongst those ships was the incomplete 34,000-ton *Columbus*, originally intended for the Norddeutscher Lloyd Line, lying at Danzig. IMM bought the *Columbus* as a partner for *Olympic*, and renamed her *Homeric*. The ship was the world's largest twin-screw vessel as well as being the biggest ship in the world propelled solely by reciprocating engines. She was also a coal burner.

Above: Vedic (1918).

Left: Southampton Docks in the 1920s with *Olympic* and *Homeric* (1913) at home among the liners on view.

Above right: Homeric was originally launched as *Columbus* for the Norddeutscher Lloyd Line and ceded to Britain as war reparation in 1919. She was bought by White Star in 1920.

Right: Homeric.

White Star Line
R.M.S. Homeric

WHITE STAR LINE.
TWIN-SCREW R.M.S "HOMERIC."
34,351 TONS.

Above: Homeric.

Left: This statue of Christopher Columbus was once displayed in *Homeric's* (ex-*Columbus*) grand stairway.

Above right: Regina (1918).

Right: Cook's Tours used *Regina* in the late 1920s for its conducted trips to Canada.

Below: Arabic[3] (1908). Originally the Norddeutscher Lloyd's *Berlin*, she was bought by White Star in 1920.

COOK'S
CONDUCTED SETTLERS PARTY
CANADA
WHITE STAR LINE

Consequently, *Homeric* was found to be too slow, with a top speed of only $18\frac{1}{2}$kt and later conversion to oil-firing raised her top speed by only 1kt. That was barely enough to make her a viable proposition.

Albert Ballin, the head of the Hamburg-Amerika Line, had ordered three huge new ships as that company's answer to White Star's '*Olympics*' and Cunard's '*Lusitania*' class vessels shortly before the war. The first two of the new ships were taken over by the Cunard Line and the United States Line, the *Imperator* becoming the *Berengaria*, and the *Vaterland* becoming the *Leviathan*. The third, *Bismarck*, was taken over by White Star and renamed *Majestic*[2].

The 16,821-ton Norddeutscher Lloyd vessel *Berlin* was taken over by White Star for use on the Liverpool to New York route in 1920, and renamed *Arabic*[3]. She had been built by Blohm & Voss 12 years before.

Transfers between shipping lines continued into the 1920s. The *Pittsburgh*, which had been built in 1922 by Harland & Wolff for the American Line, another part of IMM, was taken over by White Star before she entered service with the American Line. This 16,322-ton ship was to stay with

Left: **The cover of a 1920s White Star Line cruise brochure.**

Right: Pittsburgh **(1922).**

Below: **Cutaway view of *Majestic*[2] showing the layout of the vessel.**

WHITE STAR
LINE.
TRIPLE-SCREW S.S. "PITTSBURGH,"
16,322 TONS.

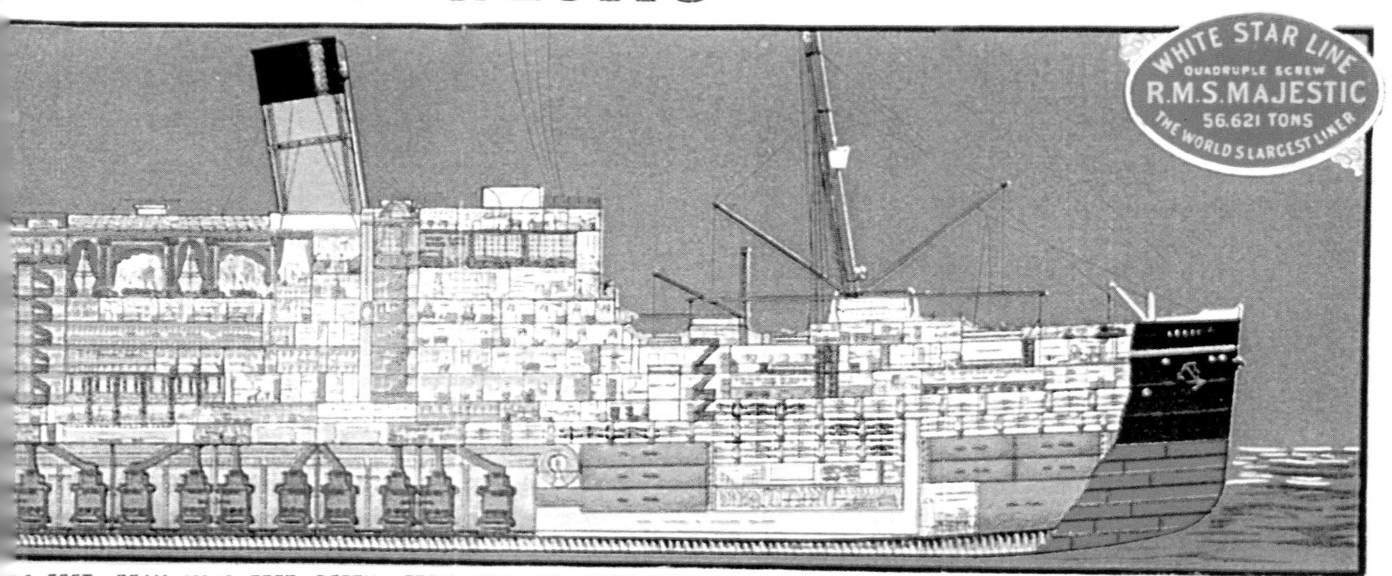
R·M·S·MAJESTIC
THE WORLD'S
LARGEST LINER
WHITE STAR LINE
QUADRUPLE SCREW
R.M.S.MAJESTIC
56.621 TONS
THE WORLD'S LARGEST LINER
-5 FEET, BEAM 100·15 FEET, DEPTH (FROM KEEL TO BOAT DECK) 101 FEET, AND TONNAGE 56,621.
WILL BE SEEN FROM THE DIAGRAMATIC PICTURE OF ITS INTERIOR.

***Left:* Majestic^{2} being eased into Southampton's Ocean Dock by tugs in 1937.**

***Centre left:* The engine room of *Majestic*^{2}.**

***Bottom and right: Doric*^{2}.**

***Bottom right: Doric*^{2} in the Mersey.**

White Star until 1925, when she was transferred to the Red Star Line and renamed *Pennland*.

The ex-German liner *Bismarck*, renamed *Majestic*^{2}, joined *Olympic* and *Homeric* on the Southampton to New York route, her maiden voyage for the White Star Line beginning on 10 May 1922. At 56,621 tons, she was the world's largest ship. On her fastest Atlantic crossing she averaged $24\frac{3}{4}$kt.

Doric^{2}, specially commissioned for the Liverpool to Montreal route, meanwhile entered service in 1922. She was the only vessel built for the White Star Line to be powered by geared turbine engines only.

During one of *Olympic*'s visits to New York, whilst backing away from New York's Pier 59 on 22 March 1924, she ran into the Furness Withy liner

WHITE STAR LINER "DORIC" (16,500 TONS).

R.M.S. "DORIC."

WHITE STAR LINE

"MAJESTIC"
THE
LARGEST STEAMER
IN THE WORLD

LENGTH – 954·5
BREADTH – 100·15
DEPTH – 64·2 FT

SOUTHAMPTON

Left: A 1922 advertising poster showing *Majestic*^{2} (1914). Originally built for the Hamburg-Amerika Line as *Bismarck*, she was ceded to Britain as war reparation in 1919 and bought by White Star in 1922.

Above: Doric (1923), shortly before leaving Liverpool for the last time in 1935.

Left: Majestic^2. The photograph is believed to date from the late 1920s.

Below: Majestic^2.

WHITE STAR LINE CRUISE

S.S. "DORIC"

THE White Star Liner "Doric" is a twin-screw steamer of 16,500 tons, is over 600 feet in length, 67 feet wide, and has a depth of 46 feet. The stern is of the Cruiser type, and the fine lines of the vessel give her a pleasing appearance at once graceful and imposing.

The very complete electrical installation on board is supplied from three main turbo generators, having a combined B.H.P. of 1,125. Everything possible has been done to ensure the comfort of passengers under all climatic conditions, including the provision of fans, ensuring ventilation in the hottest weather likely to be experienced.

The main machinery consists of two sets of Brown Curtis Single Reduction Geared Turbines, driving one port and one starboard propeller. Each set comprises one high pressure turbine which exhausts to one low pressure turbine and thence to the condenser, and the power is equivalent to about 4,500 horses, making a total for the ship of 9,000. Steam is supplied by six double-ended boilers of the multitubular cylindrical type.

The "Doric's" construction and excellent appointments have made for her a name deservedly outstanding among Britain's Cruising Liners.

The situation of the principal rooms, etc., will be found below.

PRINCIPAL PUBLIC ROOMS, &c.

BOAT DECK	SPORTS. SUN DECK.	
PROMENADE DECK	LOUNGE - DRAWING ROOM SMOKING ROOM VERANDAH GYMNASIUM COCKTAIL BAR PROMENADE SPORTS.	AMIDSHIPS AMIDSHIPS AFT AFT AFT AMIDSHIPS
A DECK	SWIMMING POOLS LADIES' AND GENTLEMEN'S HAIRDRESSER DOCTOR AND SURGERY SUITES AND STATEROOMS PROMENADE.	FORWARD AND AFT AMIDSHIPS AFT
B DECK	PURSER'S AND ENQUIRY OFFICE SHORE EXCURSION OFFICE PHOTOGRAPHERS' SHOW ROOM SMOKING ROOM BARBER'S SHOP STATEROOMS.	AMIDSHIPS AFT AFT AFT AFT
C DECK	DINING SALOON DARK ROOM STATEROOMS.	AMIDSHIPS FORWARD
D DECK	DINING SALOONS LOUNGE - STATEROOMS.	AMIDSHIPS AFT
E DECK	STATEROOMS ONLY.	

Right, clockwise: The entrance to *Majestic*[2]'s first class lounge.

The restaurant on *Majestic*[2].

The first class dining saloon of *Majestic*[2].

The first class lounge on *Majestic*[2].

The palm court restaurant on *Majestic*[2].

Fort St George. It was believed at the time that *Olympic* had escaped serious damage and so she proceeded with her voyage, but in reality the collision had broken her immense aft cast stern frame. Later repairs to *Olympic* would involve replacing the entire frame.

That year another long-standing figure in White Star's history passed away. On 7 June 1924, while aboard the Royal Mail Steamer *Ebro*, making an inspection tour of South American harbour facilities, James Pirrie collapsed and died. His body was shipped home aboard *Olympic*. He was buried in the city cemetery in Belfast and on his tomb there is a plaque with a picture of *Olympic*, and the legend: 'RMS *Olympic* 45,439 tons for the White Star Line, built by Harland & Wolff 1911'.

Before James Pirrie died Lord Kylsant had gained control of Harland & Wolff, and upon Pirrie's demise he took over as chairman. Clearly Kylsant expected the long-standing arrangement between IMM and what was now his shipbuilding yard to continue, but he was mistaken. In common with other shipowners, White Star was becoming increasingly concerned at the rising cost of building new vessels and having older ones repaired.

The seven-year-old 8,006-ton *Delphic*[2] joined the White Star from Atlantic Transport in 1925. Another vessel brought in was the *Regina*, which seems to have made occasional voyages for White Star between 1922 and 1929. The 16,500-ton *Regina* had been built as a cargo vessel in 1918 for the Dominion Line by Harland & Wolff. Despite not having been designed as a passenger ship, she served with White Star as such.

During the mid-1920s the *Laurentic*[2] was ordered from Harland & Wolff. This vessel was to

Left: Extract from *Doric's* 1934 cruise programme describing the ship.

be built to a fixed price rather than on the 'cost plus' basis usually employed, in an effort to save a little money for White Star. White Star got exactly what it paid for and the ship turned out to be a disappointment to her owner.

Alarmed by the fixed price contract to build *Laurentic*[2], Lord Kylsant began negotiating for control of the Oceanic Steam Navigation Company. Shortly afterwards it was announced that Kylsant, as chairman of the Royal Mail Steam Packet Company, had bought the White Star Line for £7 million. His first act as chairman of the line was to reinstate the 'cost plus' agreement with his own shipbuilding company, Harland & Wolff.

With the acquisition of the White Star Line, the Kylsant group of companies became, with more than two million tons of shipping, the largest shipowner in the world. The only real fly in the ointment was that Lord Kylsant and the Royal Mail Group did not have the necessary money to pay for the White Star Line.

In January 1927 a new company, White Star Line Limited, was incorporated, with Kylsant as chairman and Harold Sanderson as deputy chairman. Two and a half million

Top: _Laurentic_[2] (1927).

Right: White Star management during one of their periodic inspection tours of the line's Liverpool terminal, some time in the late 1920s. Harold Sanderson is fourth from the right in the back row.

***Left:* A lorry-load of Seville oranges leaves Liverpool's Gladstone Dock, bound for Hartley's marmalade factory, having been brought in by *Cedric*.**

£1 preference shares were issued, which raised almost four times their face value. Encouraged by the response of the first share issue by the new company, a further issue of another £2.5 million was made six months after the first. Both of these share issues were guaranteed as to capital and interest by the Royal Mail Steam Packet Company, which put that company at risk because, as we have already seen, it did not have the necessary reserves to cover the guarantee.

The new shareholders were probably unaware that when White Star Line Limited was formed £4 million in ordinary share capital was issued, but this was all subscribed to from within the Royal Mail Group, which paid only 2s (10p) on each share. Instead of raising £4 million the share issue had brought in only £400,000. Put simply, the new company's financial affairs were little more than a huge swindle.

No sooner had the Royal Mail Group taken over the Oceanic Steam Navigation Company than Lord Kylsant had himself installed as chairman. Without delay, he began to siphon off White Star profits and channel them into Royal Mail's coffers.

The 18,940-ton Royal Mail Steam Packet Company's *Ohio* joined the White Star fleet in 1927 as the *Albertic*. The 9-year-old *Orca* was also brought in during 1927, and renamed *Calgaric*. This 16,063-ton vessel had been built by Harland & Wolff for the Pacific Steam Navigation Company.

Harland & Wolff completed and handed over the new *Laurentic*[2] in 1927. She stayed with the line-up to the end of its existence and was placed in reserve in 1936. She was used on the odd occasion as a troopship and on the outbreak of war was converted for use as

***Below:* *Albertic* (1923) was originally laid down for Norddeutscher Lloyd in 1914 as *München*. Ceded to Britain, she was completed for the Royal Mail Line as *Ohio* in 1923 and later bought by White Star in 1927.**

WHITE STAR M.V. "BRITANNIC" AT LIVERPOOL.
THE LARGEST MOTOR SHIP IN THE WORLD.

Above left: *Calgaric* in the River Mersey in 1933.

Left: *Calgaric* (1918) was built as a cargo vessel for the Pacific Steam Navigation Company and named *Orca*. She was bought by White Star in 1927.

Above: *Britannic*[3] leaving Liverpool for her maiden voyage on 28 June 1930.

an armed merchant cruiser. On 3 November 1940 *Laurentic*[2] was torpedoed and sank the following day.

In 1928 a White Star liner was involved in another accident. *Celtic*[2] ran aground off Roches Point lighthouse near Queenstown at about 5am on 10 December. Although the weather had been rough, visibility was still relatively clear and the lighthouse, marking the harbour entrance, had been in full view for some time when *Celtic*[2] went aground on the Cow and Calf rocks, less than a quarter mile from it. Captain Berry immediately had the ship's whistle sounded to alert the lighthouse keeper, F. Hill, who notified the authorities and shore-based lifeboats. The passengers' luggage was transferred to the other vessels standing by as the ship was firmly aground.

It was rapidly becoming obvious that the costs of salvage and repair of the 27-year-old liner would be more than she was worth, so, on 19 December, White Star decided to salvage as much as it could from the vessel and then abandon her to her fate. The wreck was bought by the Danish shipbreaker Petersen & Albeck, and dismantled where it lay.

The first repayments of quite substantial amounts of money to the Treasury by the Royal Mail Steam Packet Company became due in 1929, with further repayments due in the next year. Lord Kylsant was unable to find the money, which was owed as the result of facilities granted under the Trade Facilities Act, so he asked the Treasury for an extension on the loans. The Treasury's Advisory Committee, under Lord Plender, decided that as the Royal Mail Group companies were so intertwined and there was so little information available as to the group's true financial status, an independent report was needed.

Sir William McLintock was instructed to look into the affairs of the Kylsant Group. McLintock's report to the Treasury in 1930 led it to the decision that an extension on the loans would not help, and that a consultation involving all those with a financial interest in the Royal Mail Group was required.

As a result of this consultation the Treasury agreed to extend the loans, but only if control of all the companies within the Royal Mail Group, including White Star, was put into the hands of three trustees.

In 1930, for the first time in its 61-year-history, the White Star Line operated at a loss. The writing was on the wall and the line would never recover from its involvement with Lord Kylsant, showing a loss for 1931, 1932 and 1933 as well.

Concern over White Star Ltd's finances brought about a Government inquiry into its affairs early in 1931. The inquiry discovered at least some of the irregularities that had occurred in

BRITANNIC

White Star Line
M.V. Britannic

Left: Britannic[3] (1930), showing the port side view.

Bottom left: Starboard view of *Britannic*[3].

Above: An aerial view of *Britannic*[3] leaving Liverpool at the start of her maiden voyage.

Left: Georgic[2] (1932), the last liner built for the White Star Line.

Below: Georgic[2] later in her life, with her dummy forward funnel removed.

1926, 1927 and 1928. On 13 May 1931 Owen Phillips – Lord Kylsant – was charged with falsifying the 1926 and 1927 annual reports and issuing false statements in the 1928 stock prospectus. Kylsant's accountant, John Morland, was charged with 'aiding, abetting and instigating Lord Kylsant in issuing false statements'.

Lord Kylsant took full responsibility for the goings-on from 1926 to 1928 and, having been found guilty of 'making, publishing and circulating' a misleading prospectus, was sentenced to one year's imprisonment. Upon his release, Lord Kylsant retired from public life, except for occasional appearances, to his home in Carmarthenshire, Wales. He died on 5 July 1937 at the age of 74.

*Georgic*² arrived in Liverpool on 13 June 1932. As hull No 896 she was the last ship to be constructed by Harland & Wolff for the White Star Line. So great had the line's difficulties become by the following year that the company began to break up into its original component parts.

White Star's losses between 1930 and 1933, coupled with the fact that the fleet was obsolete and in desperate need of modernisation or replacement, meant that the line was in great danger unless new finance was secured. Joseph Bruce Ismay (now over 70 years old) was approached by Colonel Frank Bustard, a White Star manager, to attempt to rescue the company. Ismay agreed to try, and a new board of directors was appointed, but it was already too late.

The Depression had also caused problems for White Star's great rival, Cunard. John Brown's Clydebank shipyard had laid down a new ship for Cunard late in 1930, the 81,000-ton *Queen Mary*. Shortage of funds had meant that work on the new ship had been suspended at the end of 1931. Luckily, the new Cunard super-liner had caught the public imagination and this put a certain amount of pressure on the Government to help

***Left:* The wireless room on *Georgic*² was built into her dummy forward funnel.**

***Below:* Laundry from *Britannic*³ is seen being unloaded at Liverpool in the 1930s.**

***Right:* The ship that brought about the merger between the White Star and Cunard lines – *Queen Mary*.**

QUEEN MARY

***Above and left:* In 1936 *Majestic*[2] was withdrawn from White Star service and was destined for the scrapyard when the Admiralty bought her for use as a cadet training ship. For her time with the Admiralty she was renamed *Caledonia*.**

finance the completion of the vessel.
The Treasury finally agreed, but with conditions.

The Government would advance the money to complete the *Queen Mary* only if Cunard and White Star merged. In 1934 the two lines combined, becoming Cunard-White Star. The Treasury then handed over £9.5 million to the newly united companies. Of this, £3 million was for the completion of the *Queen Mary*, £5 million was to build the *Queen Elizabeth* and £1.5 million was working capital. The Cunard-White Star fleet consisted of 25 vessels. Fifteen of these were Cunard ships, with an average tonnage of 21,951 tons per ship. The other 10 were White Star vessels weighing an average of 28,568 tons each. The merger meant the end of the Oceanic Company and its assets, and its interests in the Australian and New Zealand trade. Its ships, its property and even the office furniture were sold. What remained of the White Star fleet was almost entirely disposed of in 1934.

The year 1934 was also to presage the end of one of White Star's last great liners, the *Olympic*. It had already been an eventful year for the Nantucket lightship, moored 41 miles southeast of Nantucket Island, about 200 miles from New York. On 4 January the lightship had been sideswiped by the 24,500-ton American liner *Washington*, taking away her lifeboat davits and wireless rigging. On the night of 14 May two passing ships had nearly run her down in the fog. This was nothing unusual for the

AT NEWPORT, MONMOUTHSHIRE
Cunard White Star liner *Doric* waiting to be broken up.

Left: ***Doric*****[2] at Newport, Monmouthshire, awaiting demolition in 1935.**

Below: **A section of superstructure being removed from** ***Doric*****[2].**

lightship's crew who had taken to swinging the lifeboats out in fog, just in case. Then, at about 11 o'clock on the morning of 15 May, less than a week after the official formation of the Cunard-White Star Line, another huge dark shape loomed up out of the fog – the *Olympic*. Although the liner had already reduced speed three times during the night, first from 19½kt to 16kt, then to 12kt, and finally to about 10kt, there was still no time to avoid a collision. She was doing no more than 2kt or 3kt when she struck and crushed the lightship. *Olympic's* boats managed to rescue four of the lightship's 11-man crew. It was to signal the end of the old liner's working life.

On 25 January 1935 Cunard-White Star announced that *Olympic* would be retired at the end of the spring. She completed her last transatlantic voyage, arriving at Southampton on 12 April. Among her crew for that last round trip to New York by an '*Olympic*' class vessel was Frederick Fleet, the lookout aboard *Titanic* immediately before her fatal collision 23 years before.

White Star's head offices at 30 James Street, Liverpool, closed down on 1 September 1934. White Star Line Limited was wound up by High Court order in April 1935. In just eight years the preference and ordinary shareholders, along with other creditors, had lost over £11 million pounds. The Royal Mail Steam Packet Company, the parent company to White Star Limited, failed in February 1936, with a deficit of over £22 million.

18

Captain R.J.N. Nicholas RD RNR Commander.

Towards Cobh & New York

Day of the Month 17th September 1960

A.M.	REMARKS.
	Lights, wells, vents, lookouts tended. All fire appliances in readiness.
	1.00 Daunt Rk. 52°-33'N 5°-46'W C/C 213°
	0.33 Tuskar Lt. 000°-3.8 mls C/C 245°. 2.55 Barrels L.V. abm 335°-1.6
	3.40 Coningbeg L.V. 000°-2.2 mls C/C 255°
	Rough sea, mod N'ly swell. O'cast with rain at times. Rounds by 3/1/0
	5.30 Mine Hd Lt. 319°-11.2' C/C 258° 6.55 Ballycotton Lt. 042°-5.5' C/C 273°...
	7.01 Clocks synchronised. 7.02 S.B.E. 7.04 half ahd. 7.15 (0615Z) ARRIVAL ROCHE'S PT.
	H4EAR. off Pilot [illegible] 7.17 Stop. 7.25 Pilot boarded, the proceeding to Rds. ...
	7.43 Let go Port anchor in 57ft water. 7.56 Brought up ...
	8.0 Mod sea, O'cast with rain showers.
	8.20 Tender "BLARNEY" alongside Stbd. 8.25 Com'd embarkation 8.33 ...
	Port No. 4. 9.10 Completed embarkation. Com'd loading cargo & baggage. 9.30 Com'd loading ...
	9.55 Com'd loading Mails.
	10.30 Completed loading Car.
	11.42 Officials away, gangway landed. 11.46 Completed loading mails. S.B.E.
	11.54 Completed loading Cargo & Baggage. Tender & lighter depart.
	11.57 Com'd weighing anchor.
	Slight sea, mod swell. Mainly o'cast with rain showers. Lights taken in at Sunrise A.M.

LAT. OBD.	LONG. CHRON.	COURSE AND DIST.	VARIATION.	BEARING AND DISTANCE.

P.M.	
	12.01 Pilot away. 12.03 Anchor away. Slow ahd. H4EAR. 12.04 Swinging to Stbd.
	12.07 Swung, fixed & proceeding. 12.13 R.O.E. Full ahd. Co. V.T.M.O.
	12.15 (1115Z) DEPARTURE ROCHE'S PT. 018°-1.6 mls
	12.36 Daunt L.V. 074°-1' C/C 233° C/C 252°
	1.52 Old Head of Kinsale L.H. 325°-0.5' C/C 252°
	3.15 Fastnet Rk L.H. 258°-8 mls C/C 267° 3.43 Fastnet Rk L.H. abm 177°...
	4.0 Slight sea, low N'ly swell. O'cast & clear.
	5.30 Report of accident to E. BAIRD, Kitchenman at 1030 aft. 16th.
	7.00 Crossed 100fm line "OFF SOUNDINGS".
	Mod sea & N'ly swell. O'cast & clear.
	9.00 Chief Officer's Rounds.
	9.58 Dev. Nil. Gyro Nil.
	Slight sea, mod NW swell. Cloudy & clear. Lights hung out at Sunset P.M. Rounds by 3/1/0.

19

L.P. 39/378. 1/60.

SHIP Britannia

From Cobh

Day of the Week Sunday

A.M.	K.	F.	COURSES. Gyro	COURSES. Stand	WINDS.	BAR.	THER. AIR.	THER. WATER.	LOOK-OUTS. NAME.	LOOK-OUTS. FROM.	REV.
	16	7									
I.	16	7	267°	282°	NNW. 2						
II.	16	7									88.6
III.	16	7	263°	277°							88.0
IV.	16	7									88.4
V.	16	8			NNW 2/3	29.89	58°	59°			88.4
VI.	16	8		278							88.4
VII.	16	8	"		Lt Airs						88.2
VIII.	16	8	"	280°							88.1
IX.	16	8		"	SE'ly 2	29.88	58°	59°	White	6/8	88.1
X.	16	8									87.6
XI.	16	8									87.6
XII.	16	8	"	"	NW. 7	29.91	59°	59°			87.6

GMT NOON 1200 — COURSE. VAR. — DISTANCE. 413' — DIF. LAT. — DEP. — LAT. D.R. 50°-55'N — LONG. D.R. 19°-02'W

P.M.	K.	F.	COURSES. Gyro	COURSES. Stand	WINDS.	BAR.	THER. AIR.	THER. WATER.	LOOK-OUTS. NAME.	LOOK-OUTS. FROM.	REV.
I.	16	7	263° +2°S	283°	NW 6						
II.	16	3									
III.	16	3	260° +1°S +2°S	281°						1½/2	87.7
IV.	16	3									87.5
V.	16	3			NW. 4/5	30.08	56°	57°		3/4	87.5
VI.	16	3									87.0
VII.	16	3	"	282°						4/6	87.8
VIII.	16	3	"								87.8
IX.	16	3		"	NW. 5	30.24	56°		White		88.1

Voyage No. 273

HOLD TEMPERATURES

L.P. 22/748

	DATE		No. 1	No. 2	No. 3	No. 4	No. 5	No. 6	No. 7	No. 8
Sep '60	30th.	A.M.	78	76	–	–	74	72	–	70
		P.M.	82	80	–	–	78	76	–	74
Oct '60	1st.	A.M.	78	76	–	–	76	74	–	72
		P.M.	76	76	–	–	74	74	–	70
	2nd.	A.M.	68	68	–	–	68	70	–	66
		P.M.	66	64	–	–	66	64	–	60
	3rd.	A.M.	64	62	–	–	64	64	–	60
		P.M.	66	64	–	–	64	66	6	62
	4th.	A.M.	68	66	–	–	66	68	–	60
		P.M.	68	68	–	–	68	68	–	62
	5th.	A.M.	68	68	–	–	68	68	–	62
		P.M.	68	68	–	–	68	70	–	64
	6th.	A.M.	66	66	–	–	66	68	–	62
		P.M.	70	68	–	–	68	68	–	64

Signed [illegible signature]

62

Pages from the log book of *Britannic*[3], September 1960, shortly before her final voyage in service in November of that year.

42

M.V. "BRITANNIC" Voyage 273

PARTICULARS SAILING

	Tons
Spare Anchor and Cable	16
New Superstructure	196
Radar	2
Cargo	984
Oil Fuel	1827
Salt Water	1172
Fresh Water	2437
Stores	500
Mail	NIL
Baggage	50
Passengers	38
Crew and Effects	30
Lubricating Oil	30
Dunnage	50
Service Water	50
Grand Total :	7382
Calculated Dead Weight	7382
Dead Weight per scale	7439
Difference	57
Draft Forward	29'00"
„ Aft	28'08"
„ Mean	28'10"
Density	1006
Fresh Water Allowance	7"

PASSENGERS

First Class	NIL
Tourist Class	547
Total :	547

CREW

Deck	72
Engine	58
Catering	206
Total :	336
Total on Board :	883

MAIL

Mail: Registered	NIL
„ Letter	
„ P.P.	
„ Embassy	
„ Fleet	
Total:	

Specie NIL

G.M. 3.36 Ft.

[signature] Chief Officer

Above: Liverpool in 1948, showing areas of World War 2 bomb damage. The White Star office building (just left of centre) appears to have completely escaped the attention of the Luftwaffe.

Above right: _Britannic_[3] – the last vessel to cross the Atlantic under the White Star Line flag.

Below: Label on the front cover of a log book from _Britannic_[3], 1960.

On 20 August 1935 Cunard-White Star announced that prospective breakers could inspect *Olympic* on the following Monday. She was bought for £100,000 by Sir John Jarvis, who quickly sold her on to Thomas W. Ward Ltd, of Inverkeithing, with the stipulation that she would be broken up at Jarrow, an area badly affected by the Depression. *Olympic* arrived at Jarrow on 13 October and what had been probably the most successful of all the ships to have sailed for the White Star Line began to be dismantled on 6 November. Fixtures and fittings from the ship were auctioned aboard.

Majestic[2] was also sold to Thomas W. Ward Ltd for scrapping in May 1936, but this was not the end for the ex-German *Bismarck*. In June Ward's sold *Majestic* to the Admiralty and she was converted into the training ship HMS *Caledonia*. On 29 September 1939 she was destroyed by fire while at Rosyth, Scotland, and sank at her berth. By the time Cunard had finished weeding out what White Star ships it did not want, only three remained: *Britannic*[3], *Laurentic*[2] and *Georgic*[2].

On Sunday October 17 1937 Joseph Bruce Ismay died at his Hill Street home in London, three days after suffering a stroke that had taken his sight and speech. By the close of 1937 all that remained of the once great Oceanic Steam Navigation Company was a small office in Cockspur Street, Liverpool. Even that was eventually closed when the last of its

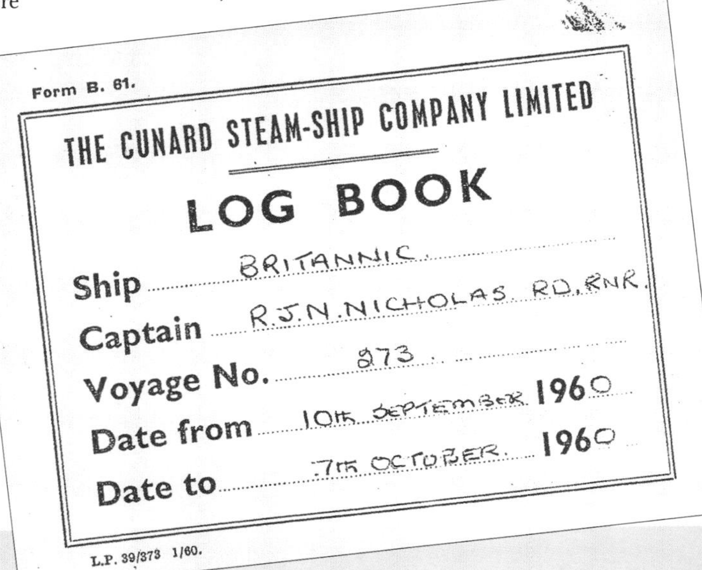
Form B. 61.

THE CUNARD STEAM-SHIP COMPANY LIMITED

LOG BOOK

Ship BRITANNIC

Captain R.J.N. NICHOLAS RD, RNR

Voyage No. 273

Date from 10th SEPTEMBER 1960

Date to 7th OCTOBER 1960

L.P. 39/373 1/60.

furniture and carpets was sold at auction. In all but name the White Star Line had ceased to exist. The Oceanic Steam Navigation Company was wound up on 21 August 1939, less than a fortnight before the outbreak of World War 2.

In the late spring of 1940 *Georgic*[2] was requisitioned for use as a troopship. She was equipped to carry over 5,000 troops, more than three times her peacetime capacity, and was painted battleship grey. On 14 July 1941, as she lay anchored in Port Tewfik, at the southern end of the Suez Canal, Egypt, *Georgic*[2] was attacked by German bombers. A near miss caused severe damage and No 4 hold began to flood. Then a second bomb struck the after deck and exploded deep within the ship, causing serious fires. *Georgic*[2] was beached on North Reef, the passengers and crew taken off, and the ship was allowed to burn herself out.

The burned-out shell of *Georgic*[2] was subsequently raised and towed to Port Sudan, where she could be patched up. She arrived there on 10 January 1942. After seven weeks of patching, *Georgic*[2] was towed first to Karachi and then to Bombay for extensive repairs. She reached Karachi on 1 April, and Indian workers swarmed aboard. The Indian workmen soon had the ship's machinery operational and her own electrical generators on line. On 11 December the battered vessel sailed, under her own power, for Bombay and to begin five weeks of repair work on her hull.

She arrived at Bombay on 13 December 1942, and left on 20 January 1943 after hull repairs were completed. *Georgic*[2] arrived back in the Mersey on 1 March 1943 with 5,000 tons of pig iron aboard as cargo. After yet another inspection, the Ministry of War Transport and the Admiralty decided to convert *Georgic*[2] into a dedicated troopship. She re-entered service on 14 December 1944.

In 1947 the Cunard Steam Ship Company bought all that remained of Cunard-White Star share capital. From then onwards the White Star Line was wholly owned by Cunard and the name was systematically phased out. In 1949 Cunard announced that it was taking over all assets and operations of the Cunard-White Star Line Ltd, and that it was dropping the White Star part of the name. However, the remaining White Star ships, *Georgic*[2] and *Britannic*[3], were allowed to keep their old company's colours.

Georgic's penultimate voyage ended on 19 November 1955 when she arrived at Liverpool with 800 soldiers aboard, from Hong Kong. The next time she left port it would be for a one-way trip to the breaker's yard.

As *Britannic*[3], the very last White Star liner, was leaving New York for the final time on 25 November 1960, one of the city's fireboats saluted her passing by sending up fountains of water from the hoses, a ceremony otherwise reserved for ships completing their maiden voyage. She arrived back at Liverpool on 4 December.

It was the end of what had once been one of the greatest shipping lines of them all: White Star.

Right: Many valuables, including gold bullion, were shipped across the Atlantic aboard White Star vessels. Here vehicles of the Dominion Express security company wait to have their load taken aboard a liner.

Below: The mail arriving at, and leaving, a White Star liner c1912.

To
GREET
YOU
AT
CHRISTMAS

Above: The Ocean Dock, Southampton, in 1920. Home to many of White Star's largest liners.

Below: Canada Dock, Liverpool, in the 1920s. The vessel nearest is *Celtic*[2] and behind her is *Baltic*[2].

Right: A Christmas card from the *Laurentic*[1] dated about 1910.

HANDS CLASPED
ACROSS THE SEA.
I can see the great ships go,
Swinging out-ward in the bay,
This by them I send to shew
I remember you to-day.
XMAS WISHES.
A.E.P.

Left: A 1920s Christmas card from the *Albertic* (1927).

Above right: A 1913 map from a White Star brochure, showing the cruise routes of the *Laurentic* and *Megantic*.

Right: Liverpool pierhead in the 1920s with a Cunard tender in the foreground.

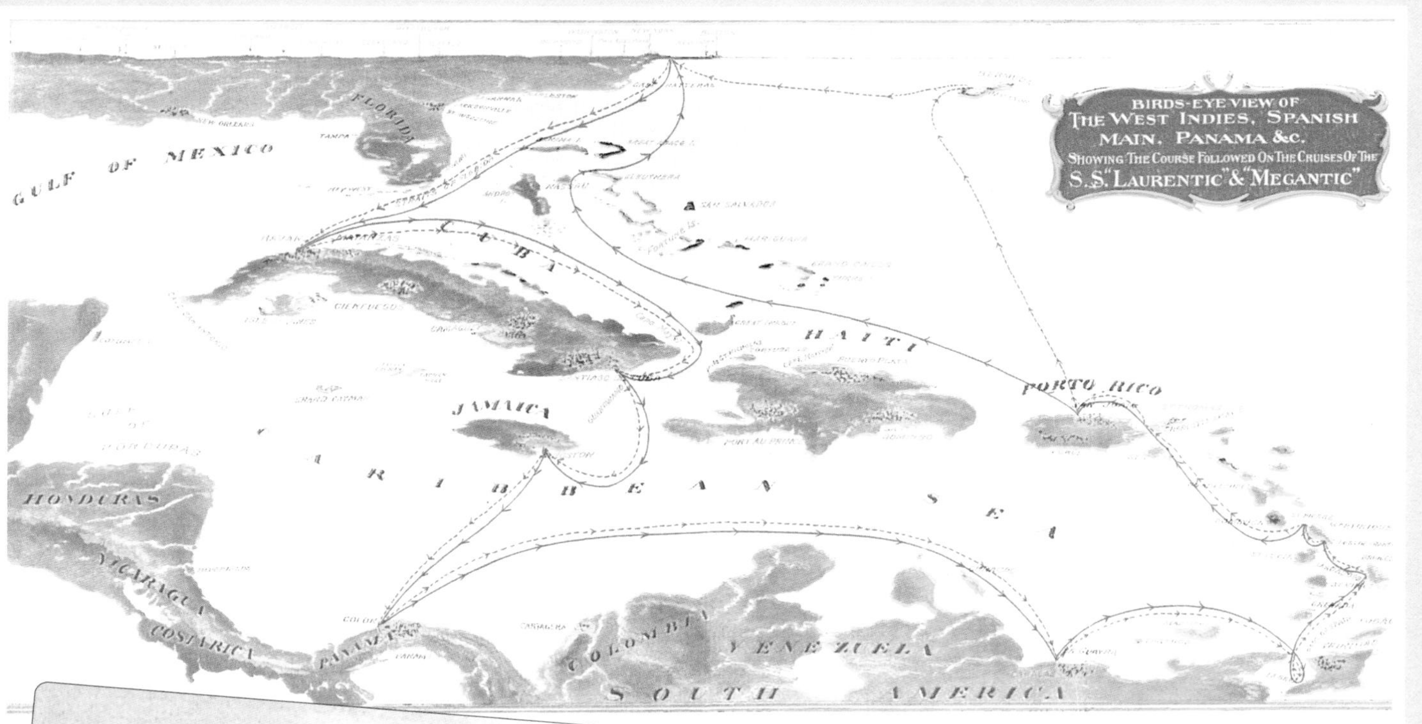
BIRDS-EYE VIEW OF
THE WEST INDIES, SPANISH
MAIN, PANAMA &c.
SHOWING THE COURSE FOLLOWED ON THE CRUISES OF THE
S.S. "LAURENTIC" & "MEGANTIC"
GULF OF MEXICO
FLORIDA
CUBA
HAITI
PORTO RICO
JAMAICA
CARIBBEAN SEA
HONDURAS
NICARAGUA
COSTARICA
PANAMA
COLOMBIA
VENEZUELA
SOUTH AMERICA

LIVER, CUNARD AND DOCK OFFICES, LIVERPOOL.
7891

THE MEDIT

PALMA. Chief port of the Balearic Isles, Palma still retains many narrow shaded streets overhung by graceful balconies indicating its Moorish origin. An excursion is run across the island to Soller, with its inland bay, fringed with waving palms, which passes this beautiful view of Miramar.

MONACO owes its fame to the fact that it is the port for Monte Carlo, and the casino has drawn clients from all parts of the world. The scenery is extremely beautiful and the view from the casino terrace is particularly fine.

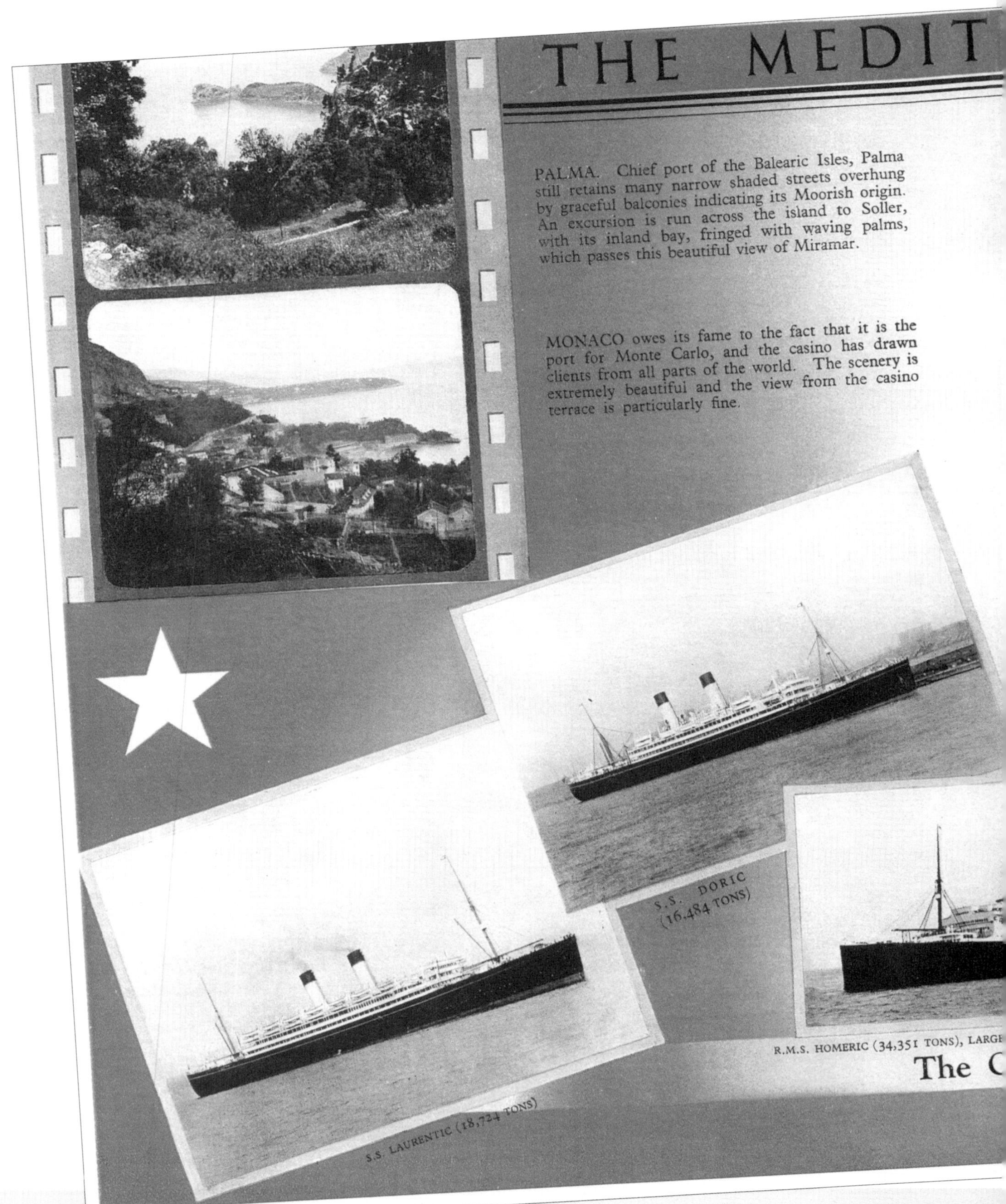

S.S. DORIC (16,484 TONS)

S.S. LAURENTIC (18,724 TONS)

R.M.S. HOMERIC (34,351 TONS), LARGE

The C

RANEAN
FANCY DRESS BALL. Who's that in the Turk's
ress ? . . . Isn't it amazing what a little make-up
will do ? . . . I should never have recognised my
ister if I hadn't seen her get that hat from the
Barber. . . . That man's a genius !
TEA ON DECK. Tea on deck—magic words !
All the joys of picnicking with none of the dis-
comforts. There are no wasps lurking out of sight
ready to pounce on the jam, no fear of a sudden shower
to wreck the tea-party, and plenty of stewards ready
close by to replenish the teapot.
S.S. ADRIATIC
24,679 TONS)
ULARLY CRUISING FROM THIS COUNTRY
g Fleet
S.S. CALGARIC (16,063 TONS)

Left: **Centrefold from a 1920s White Star cruise brochure.**

The Dear Home Land
Greeting.
HANDS ACROSS THE SEA.

FLOATING DOCK.

Top left: An advertising postcard from the Edwardian era, sold in Queenstown, Ireland, to encourage emigration to the US.

Far left: The White Star floating dock at Liverpool early in the 20th century.

Left: The cover of a brochure advertising the 1913 winter cruises of *Laurentic* and *Megantic*.

Above: Menu covers from a 1920s cruise.

Left: The White Star Line head office in James Street, Liverpool, in 1924.

Right: An illustration taken from a White Star cruise programme.

Top right: Liverpool's Gladstone Dock in 1927 with three White Star liners in evidence: *Adriatic*[1], *Megantic*, and *Delphic*[2] (1925).

Far right: Majestic[2] entering the King George V drydock at Southampton in 1928.

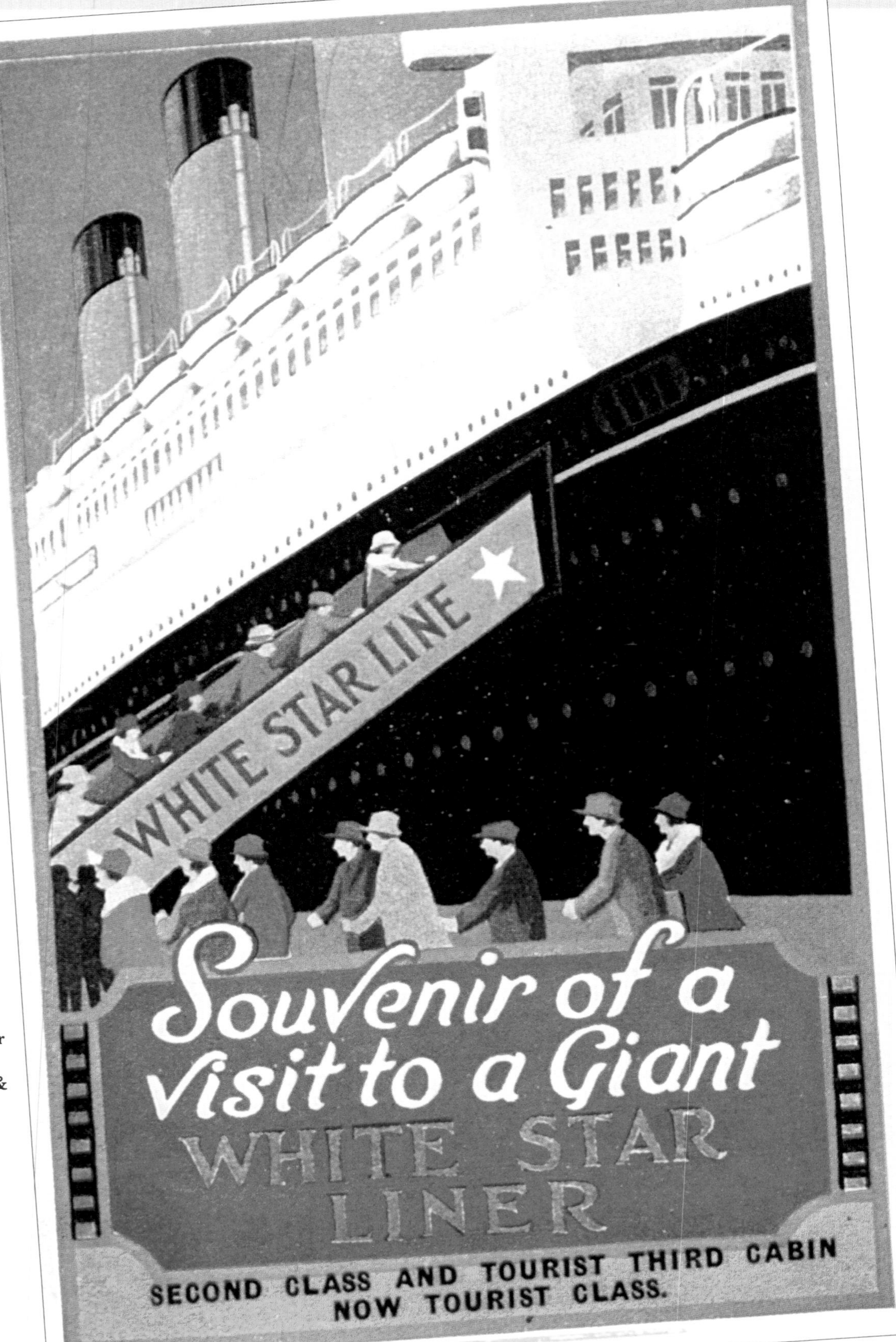

Right: White Star Line brochure from the 1920s.

Top right: *Haverford* (1901). After use a troop-carrier during World War 1, she was transferred to White Star by IMM in 1921.

Far right: The River Lagan, Belfast, opposite Harland & Wolff's shipyard.

WHITE STAR
LINE.
TWIN-SCREW S.S. "HAVERFORD."
11,635 TONS.
MONTAGUE B. BLACK
R.595.
DONEGALL QUAY, BELFAST.

The Heart of the World.

Aerial View of Manhattan Island
Showing New York Skyscrapers.

©FAIRCHILD A.C.CORP.

Above: Native Americans visiting Europe aboard *Baltic*[2] in the 1920s. Some members of this group of Arapahos fought against General George Armstrong Custer's 7th Cavalry at the battle of the Little Bighorn in 1876.

Left: A postcard of New York, White Star's main western terminal.

Right: A list of White Star's principal offices and agencies.

WHITE STAR LINE

OFFICES AND AGENCIES
AT PRINCIPAL POINTS AND PORTS OF CALL

LONDON	1, Cockspur Street, S.W.1	*Telephone :* Whitehall 1080. *Tel. Add. : Vessels Lesquare*
	36, Leadenhall Street, E.C.3	*Telephone :* Monument 0915. *Tel. Add. : Whistar Fen*
LIVERPOOL	30, James Street	*Telephone :* Bank 933. *Tel. Add. : Oceanic*
SOUTHAMPTON	Canute Road	*Telephone :* 5111. *Tel. Add. : Vessels*
BELFAST	31/33, Victoria Street	*Telephone :* 4255/6. *Tel. Add. : Vessels*
BIRMINGHAM, 2	6, Victoria Square	*Telephone :* Midland 5405/6/7. *Tel. Add. : Vessels*
COBH	Scott & Co. (Q'town), Ltd.	*Telephone :* 3. *Tel. Add. : Oceanic*
DUBLIN	1 and 2, Eden Quay	*Telephone :* 44031. *Tel. Add. : Oceanic*
GLASGOW	4, Bothwell Street	*Telephone :* Central 544. *Tel. Add. : Whitstar*
IMMINGHAM	McGregor, Gow & Holland, Ltd., Alexandra House, Docks	*Tel. Add. : Macgregor*
LEITH	A. McIntosh & Co., 41, Constitution Street	*Tel. Add. : Dunedin*
MANCHESTER	74, Cross Street	*Telephone :* Blackfriars 4301. *Tel. Add. : Vessels*
PARIS	American Travel & T'port Agency, 9, Rue Scribe	*Tel. Add. : Vessels 96*
ALEXANDRIA	John Ross & Co., Office Marina	*Tel. Add. : Ross*
Do.	L. Enokian & Co., 3, Midan Saad, Zagloul	*Tel. Add. : Lenoki*
ALGIERS	E. Delacroix & Fils, 1, Rue Calbert	*Tel. Add. : Delacroix*
AZORES	Nicholls, Raposo & Co., Ponta Delgada	*Tel. Add. : Oceanic, Ponta Delgada*
BARCELONA	MacAndrews, Edificio Colon, Paseo de Colon, 24	*Tel Add. : MacAndrews*
BERGEN	Ivar Grotte, Steamship Agent	*Tel. Add. : Passenger*
BREMEN	White Star Line, 27/28, Bahnhofstrasse	*Tel. Add. : Olympic*
BERLIN, W.8	Unter den Linden, 3a	*Tel. Add. : Traveler*
BRIDGETOWN (Barbados)	—Da Costa & Co., Ltd. (P.O. Box 103)	*Tel. Add. : Dacosta*
CADIZ	Daniel MacPherson & Co.	*Tel. Add. : MacPherson*
CAIRO	Thos. Cook & Son, Ltd., near Shepheard's Hotel	*Tel. Add. : Cook*
CASABLANCA	Cie Charbonnière de Casablanca, P.O. Box 46	*Tel. Add. : Coaling, Casablanca Maroc*
CEUTA	Jose Trujillo Zafra, Apartado de Correos Num 4	*Tel. Add. : Trujillo*
CHERBOURG	American Travel & Transport Agency, Quai Alexandre III, No. 32	*Tel. Add. : Oceanic*
COLON	W. Andrews & Co.	*Tel. Add. : Andrews*
COPENHAGEN	C. Mogensen, 1, Nyhavn	*Tel. Add. : Travel*
CRISTOBAL	W. Andrews & Co.	*Tel. Add. : Andrews*
DANZIG (Zoppot)	White Star Line, 32, Topfergasse	*Tel. Add. : Olympic*
GIBRALTAR	Thomas Mosley & Co., 74, Irish Town	*Tel. Add. : Mosley*
HAIFA	L. Alonzo & Sons	*Tel. Add. : Alonzo*
HAMBURG	Falck & Co., Glockengiesserwall 18	*Tel. Add. : Falkom*
HAVANA	West Indies Shipping & Trading Co., Apartado (P.O. Box 138)	*Tel. Add. : Westship*
HAVRE	Langstaff, Erembert & Co., 67, Quai de S'hampton	*Tel. Add. : Langstaff*
KINGSTON	Royal Mail Lines, Ltd., 8, Port Royal St., Jamaica	*Tel. Add. : Roymailine*
LA GUAIRA	A. Wallis Sucrs.	*Tel. Add. : Albis*
LAS PALMAS	Elder Dempster (Grand Canary), Ltd.	*Tel. Add. : Elder*
LISBON	Germano Serrao Arnaud, Avenida 24 de Julho No. 2	*Tel. Add. : Geranaud*
MADEIRA	Blandy Bros. & Co., Ltd., Funchal	*Tel. Add. : Blandy, Funchal*
MALAGA	MacAndrews & Co., Ltd., Lorenzo Cendra 8, Apartado 135	*Tel. Add. : MacAndrews*
MARSEILLES	L. Desbois & A. Cabaud, 80, Rue de la République	*Tel. Add. : Buenos*
MONACO	Voyages Kuoni, 3, Boulevard Victor-Hugo, Nice	*Tel. Add. : Vessels*
NAPLES	Di Luggo Wood & Co., 41/43, Via Agostino Depretis	*Tel. Add. : Oceanic*
NASSAU	R. H. Curry & Co., 303, Bay Street (P.O. Box 168)	*Tel. Add. : Curryson*
OSLO	Ferd. J. Elster & M. R. Raffel, Prinsensgade, 2c	*Tel. Add. : Passenger*
PALMA	Gabriel Mulet e Hijos, Ltd., Av. Antonio Maura 62, Palma de Mallorca	*Tel. Add. : Gamulet, Palma de Mallorca*
STOCKHOLM	A. B. Nyman & Schultz, Kungstradgardsgatan 2a	*Tel. Add. : Passenger*
TANGIER	J. G. Chappory, Hotel Cecil Building	*Tel. Add. : Chappory*
Do.	Thomas Mosley & Co., Bland House	*Tel. Add. : Marland*
TENERIFFE	Hamilton & Co.	*Tel. Add. : Hamilton*
TRINIDAD (Port of Spain and La Brea)	—Royal Mail Lines, Ltd., Port of Spain	*Tel. Add. : Roymailine, Port of Spain*
TRONDHJEM	Olaf H. Solem and Son A/s, Olaf, Trygvesons, Gate 12	*Tel. Add. : Passenger*
VIGO	Sobrinos de Jose Pastor, Ltd., Edificio Pastor	*Tel. Add. : Pastor*
VILLEFRANCHE	C. M. Powilewicz, Quai Lunel 20, Nice	*Tel. Add. : Navigation, Nice*

And all Offices of Messrs. Thos. Cook & Son, Ltd., The American Express Company, the International Sleeping Car Company, the Raymond & Whitcomb Co., Dean & Dawson, Ltd., Frames' Tours, Ltd., Pickfords, Ltd., and other Tourist Agencies throughout the World.

G.C.B. I.

The Baynard Press

Below and bottom: **Brochure advertising 1934 cruises by the *Homeric*, *Doric*^{2}, *Laurentic*^{2} and *Adriatic*^{2}.**

'HOMERIC' CRUISES

35,000 TONS

Date 1934	Itinerary	From	Days	Min. Fare
Mar. 24	Gibraltar, Barcelona, Monaco, Ajaccio, Algiers, Tangier (Easter Cruise)	Southampton	14	£25
June 16	Tangier, Algiers, Naples, Syracuse, Cattaro, Venice, Ragusa, Malta, Gibraltar	Southampton	21	32 gns.
July 14	Barcelona, Naples, Athens, Rhodes, Malta, Tangier	Southampton	19	30 gns.
Aug. 4	Madeira, Teneriffe, Las Palmas, Tangier, Lisbon (August Bank Holiday Cruise)	Southampton	14	23 gns
Aug. 22	Tangier, Palma, Naples, Messina, Gibraltar	Southampton	14	23 gns
Sept. 8	Gibraltar, Malta, Athens, Rhodes, Katakola (for Olympia), Naples, Algiers	Southampton	19	30 gns.
Sept. 29	Tangier, Malta, Mudros, Istanbul (Constantinople), Athens, Naples, Palma	Southampton	21	32 gns.

WHITE STAR LINE

'DORIC' CRUISES

16,500 TONS

Date 1934	Itinerary	From	Days	Min. Fare
Mar. 29	Lisbon, Barcelona, Palma, Ceuta (Scholars' Easter Cruise)	Liverpool ...	14	Adults 16 gns. Girls 12 .. Boys 10 ..
April 17	Gibraltar, Civita Vecchia (for Rome), Malaga, Tangier, Gibraltar	Liverpool ...	16	£15
May 18	Gibraltar, Tangier, Lisbon (Whitsuntide Cruise)	Liverpool ...	10	£10
June 2	Madeira, Teneriffe, Las Palmas, Casablanca	Liverpool ...	14	£13
June 23	Passing Gibraltar Rock, Barcelona, Monaco, Palma (*Under the auspices of the Civil Service Sports Council*)	Liverpool ...	14	£13
July 14 / 15	Greenock, Oban, Eidfjord, Ulvik, Eidfjord, Trondheim, Ole, Hellesylt, Merok, Gudvangen, Mundal, Balholm, Bergen, Leith, Immingham	Liverpool / Greenock	13	£13
July 28	Oslo, Copenhagen, Zoppot, Tallinn, Stockholm, Holtenau, Brunsbuttel, Hamburg, Southampton	Immingham	15	£15
Aug. 15	Madeira, Las Palmas, Casablanca, Lisbon (Scholars' Summer Cruise)	Southampton	13	Adults 16 gns. Girls 12 .. Boys 10 ..
Sept. 1	Lisbon, Palma, Algiers, Gibraltar	Southampton	13	£13
Sept. 15	Madeira, Teneriffe, Las Palmas, Casablanca, Gibraltar	Southampton	14	£13
Oct. 2	Barcelona, Monaco, Ceuta, Liverpool	Southampton	14	£13

WHITE STAR LINE

'LAURENTIC' CRUISE

19,000 TONS

Date	Itinerary	From	Days	Min. Fare
Mar. 23	Dublin, Gibraltar, Civita Vecchia, Palma, Ceuta, Dublin (*For Rome*) (*Under Charter to Hewitt's Travel Agency*)	Liverpool / Dublin	19	24 gns

'ADRIATIC' CRUISES

25,000 TONS

Date	Itinerary	From	Days	Min. Fare
Mar. 29	Gibraltar, Villefranche, Valetta, Algiers, Lisbon (Scouters' and Guiders' Easter Cruise)	Liverpool	17	19 gns
Aug. 4	Lisbon, Tangier, Teneriffe, Madeira (*Under Charter to National Tours, Ltd.*)	Liverpool	14	16 gns
Aug. 25	Lisbon, Algiers, Malta, Messina, Naples, Barcelona, Gibraltar (*Under Charter to National Tours, Ltd.*)	Liverpool	19	23 gns
Sept. 18	Lisbon, Algiers, Palma, Barcelona, Gibraltar, Corunna (*Under Charter to National Tours, Ltd.*)	Liverpool	15	16 gns.

EACH CRUISE ONE CLASS ONLY.

Apply **WHITE STAR LINE**

London, Belfast, Birmingham, Cobh, Dublin, Glasgow, Liverpool, Manchester, Southampton and Local Agents

PRINTED IN ENGLAND

HOLIDAYS
A PANORAMA OF NEW YORK FROM THE AIR
FROM
£34 : 10 : 0
RETURN OCEAN FARE

NOW FOR

AN ATLANTIC CRUISE TO AMERICA

FOR

PLEASURE HEALTH
INTEREST BUSINESS
SEA VOYAGE

FROM £34 : 10 : O RETURN

REDUCED OCEAN FARES BY WHITE STAR LINERS

	One-Way	Round-Trip
First Class from	£53 10 0	£107 0 0
Cabin Class from	£30 0 0	£56 0 0
Tourist Class from	£25 0 0	£44 5 0
Third Class from	£19 0 0	£34 10 0

APPLY—

WHITE STAR LINE

OFFICES OR AGENTS

NOW VISIT AMERICA

FROM £34:10:0 RETURN

WHITE STAR LINE

VISIT AMERICA

WHY?

To see your friends and relatives.
To establish business contacts.
To view the Wonders of the Western World.

WHO?

The Tourist.
The Holiday-maker.
The Business Man.

WHEN?

Any time.
Why not now?
You can do it in three weeks or even a fortnight by

SPECIAL EXCURSION SAILINGS

in the World's Largest Liner, R.M.S. "Majestic," or her Giant Sister, R.M.S. "Olympic."

TO NEW YORK AND BACK IN A FORTNIGHT

OCEAN FARE £36 : 15 : 0 RETURN

WHITE STAR LINE

Above and left: **A 1920 brochure advertising White Star Atlantic cruises to the US aboard *Majestic* and *Olympic*.**

Right: **Photographs from a 1920s White Star cruise brochure, showing just how well some people adjusted to life on board ship.**

Below: **First class menu from White Star liner *Celtic*[2] in 1928.**

MENU

S.S. "CELTIC" June 24th, 1928

Consomme Columbine — Cream of Asparagus

Poached Turbot, Bordelaise

Mutton Cutlets, Toscane

Prime Ribs and Sirloin of Beef, Yorkshire Pudding

French Beans — Patna Rice

Boiled and Browned Potatoes

Roast Chicken a l' Ivoire

Salade Cœur de Romaine

Victoria Pudding — Peach Montrose

Ice Cream and Wafers

Dessert

Tea — Coffee

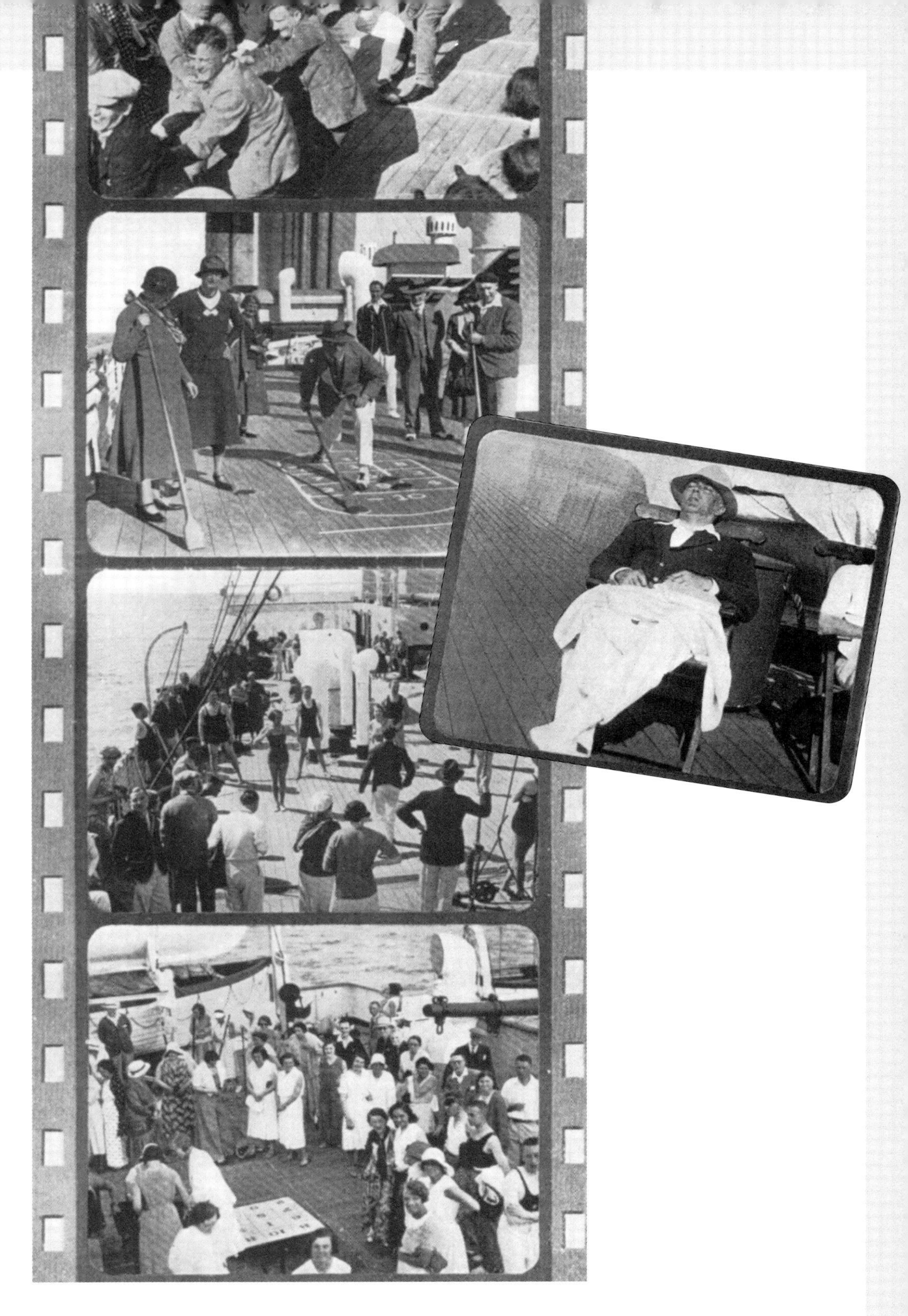

WHITE STAR LINE

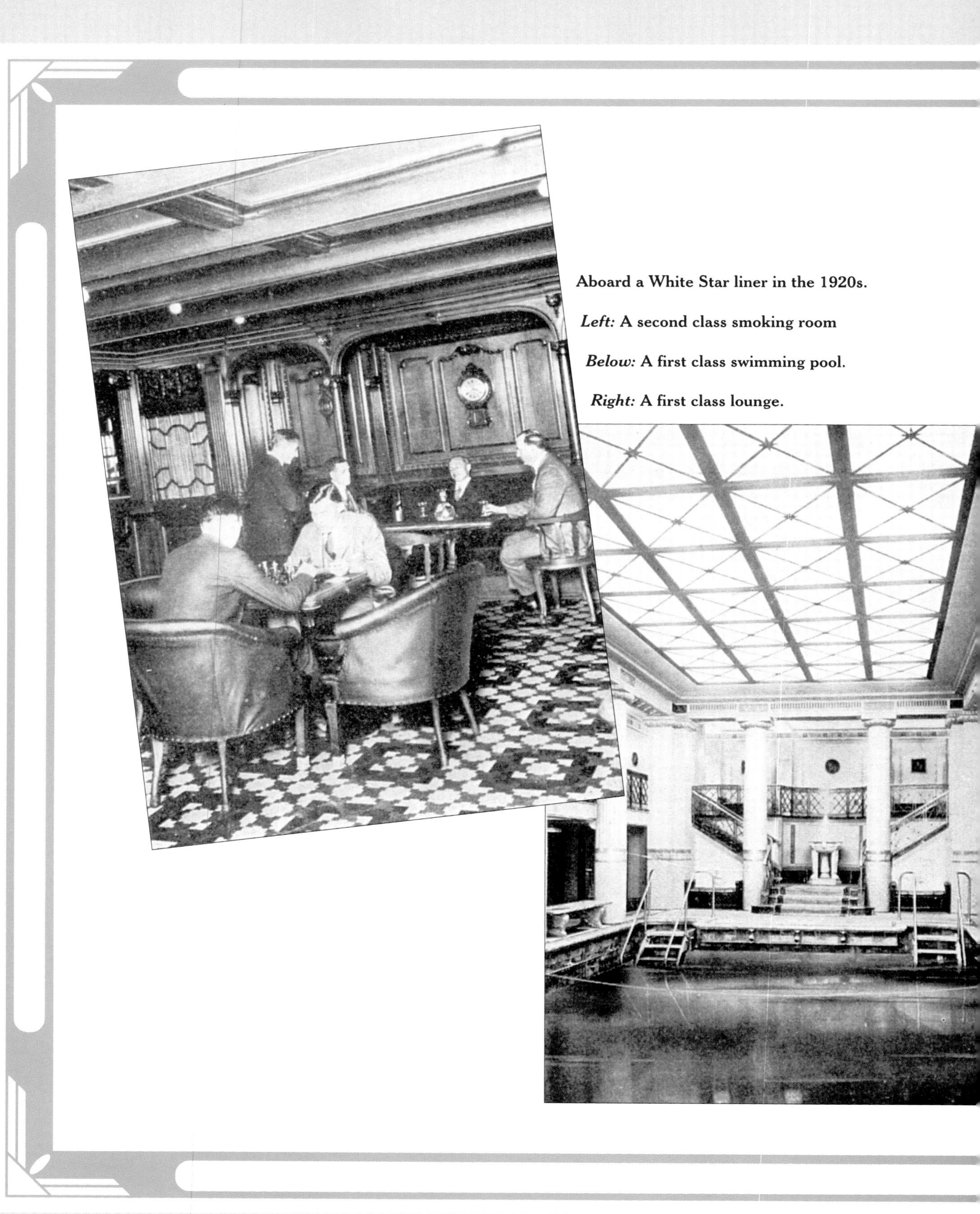

Aboard a White Star liner in the 1920s.

Left: A second class smoking room

Below: A first class swimming pool.

Right: A first class lounge.

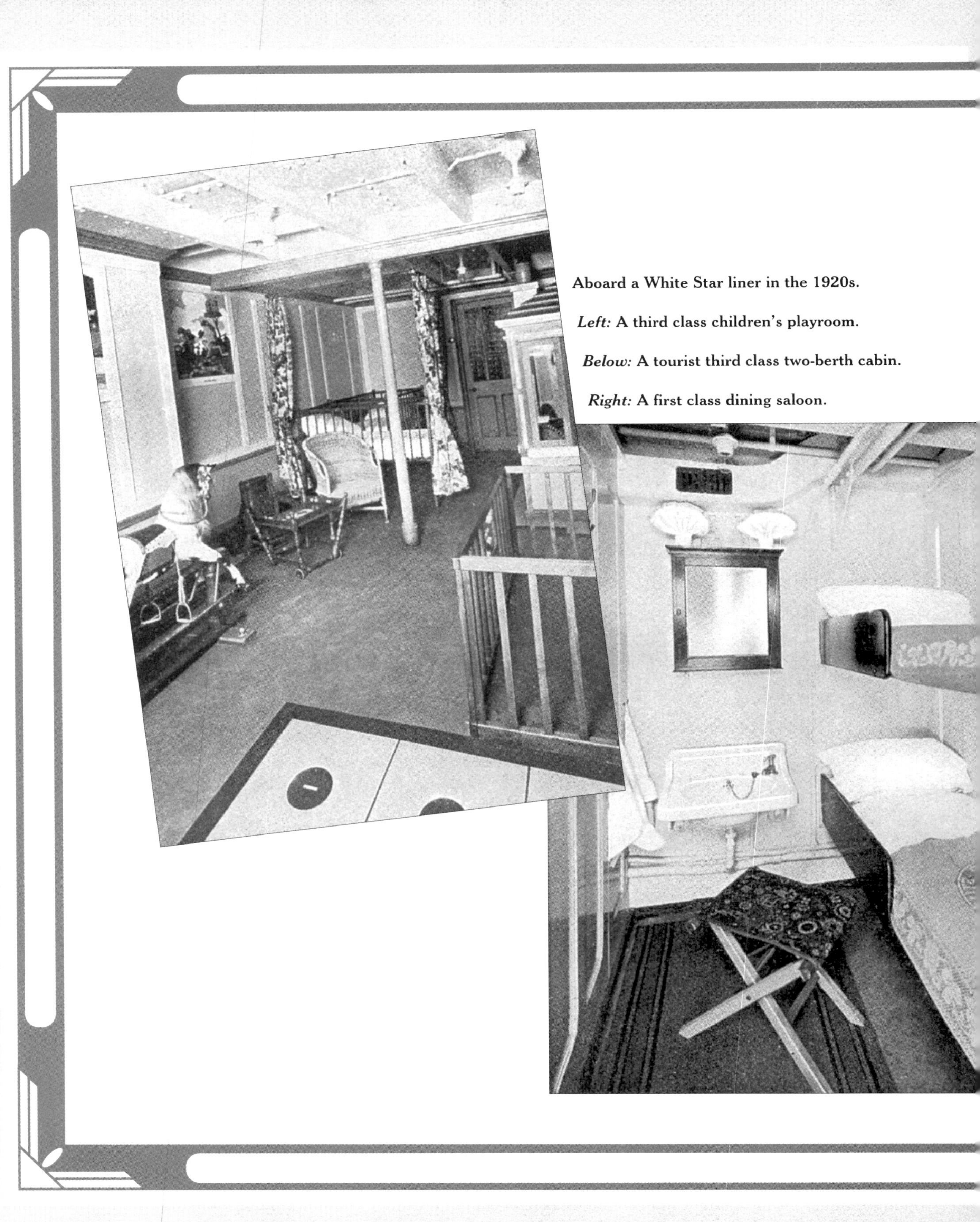

Aboard a White Star liner in the 1920s.

Left: A third class children's playroom.

Below: A tourist third class two-berth cabin.

Right: A first class dining saloon.

Left: Liverpool waterfront in 1930. The vessel top left appears to be *Britannic*[3] setting out on her maiden voyage.

Right: Liverpool waterfront and docks in 1933.

Souvenir
of a
White Star Line Cruise

Left: The cover of a souvenir copy of a 1934 White Star Line cruise programme.

Below: A postwar Cunard-White Star tourist class meal ticket.

Bottom: A Cunard-White Star luggage label.

TOURIST CLASS

SINGLE SITTING

Table No. 26

Please retain this card and present to Table Waiter

Name.................................

CUNARD WHITE STAR

MR. ARTHUR. SCOTT.

TOURIST CLASS PASSENGER PER ASCANIA. (NAME OF SHIP)

SAILING FROM HALIFAX. (PORT OF EMBARKATION) TO LIVERPOOL (PORT OF LANDING)

SAILING FEB 6th/48. ROOM No D.51

CUNARD WHITE STAR

CUNARD WHITE STAR

THURSDAY, July 26th

Deck Games ... ... 10-30 a.m.
Orchestra, Main Companion ... ... 11-0 a.m.
"Tote" on Ship's Run ... 11-0 to 12 Noon
Arrive **Leith** ... ... 4-0 p.m.
Leave **Leith** ... ... 5-0 p.m.
Diner d'Adieu ... ... 6-30 and 7-45 p.m.
Cinema in Main Lounge ... 7-30 & 9-40 p.m.
Dancing on Deck ... . 9-0 p.m.

FRIDAY, July 27th.

Arrive **Immingham** ... ... 9-0 a.m.

Subject to Alterations. Please Watch Blackboards

S.S. "DORIC," WHITE STAR LINE,
Commander; J. McROSTIE.

Summer Cruise

From LIVERPOOL, JULY 14th, 1934.

Proposed

Entertainment Programme.

Chairman: Mr. N. CALVERT.

Joint Secretaries:
Mr. H. STOWELL-BROWN
and Mr. W. E. RICHARDS

Treasurer: Mr. J. GREENHALGH

COMMITTEE:

Miss D. F. VIDAL — Mr. A. BENNETT
Mrs. E. E. CRAWFORD — Mr. W. G. GILLESPIE
Miss J. PADWICK — Mr. G. H. MUNDY
Miss M. GREENSLADE — Mr. W. N. HART
Miss M. WALKER — Mr. J. D. TAYLOR
Miss G. CANNING — Mr. Z. VIDOR

TOURNAMENTS IN CHARGE OF:

DECK TENNIS: Miss J. Padwick, Mrs. E. Crawford, Mr. G. H. Mundy, Mr. J. D. Taylor
...OARD: Miss D. F. Vidal, Miss M. Walker, Mr. W. N. Hart, Mr. Z. Vidor
...: Miss M. Greenslade, Miss G. Canning, Mr. A. Bennett, Mr. J. Greenhalgh
...Mr. W. E. Richards and Miss E. Kershaw

Right and below: Programme for the 1934 summer cruise of the *Doric*.

Bottom right: **A Cunard-White Star voucher showing the rate of exchange for US dollars to pounds sterling in February 1948.**

SS Doric 14/7/34

Programme of Events.

SATURDAY, July 14th.

Leave **Liverpool** ... ... 7-0 p.m.
Get-together Dance on Deck ... ... 9-0 p.m.

SUNDAY, July 15th.

Divine Service in Main Lounge ... ... 11-0 a.m.
Arrive **Greenock** ... ... 12 Noon
Leave **Greenock** ... ... 2-0 p.m.
Orchestra, Main Companion ... ... 4-0 p.m.
Cinema in Main Lounge ... 7-30 & 9-40 p.m.
Dancing, on Promenade Deck ... ... 9-0 p.m.

MONDAY, July 16th.

Arrive **Oban** ... ... 7-0 a.m.
Leave **Oban** ... ... 5-0 p.m.
Dancing on Deck ... ... 9-0 p.m.

TUESDAY, July 17th.

Meeting to Select Sports' Committee, in Drawing Room ... 10-30 a.m.
Orchestra, Main Companion ... ... 11-0 a.m.
"Tote" on Ship's Run, (A Deck Aft) 11-0 to 12 Noon
Horse Races, on Sports Deck Aft ... 2-30 p.m.
Orchestra, Main Companion ... ... 4-0 p.m.
Gala Dinner and Dance ... 6-30 & 7-45 p.m.
Cinema in Lounge ... ... 7-30 & 9-40 p.m.

WEDNESDAY, July 18th.

Arrive **Eidfjord** ... ... 8-0 a.m.
Leave **Eidfjord** ... ... 9-30 a.m.
Arrive **Ulvik** ... ... 5-0 p.m.
Leave **Ulvik** ... ... 6-0 p.m.
Arrive **Eidfjord** ... ... 9-0 p.m.
Whist Drive in "D" Deck Lounge ... 9-0 p.m.
Dancing on Deck

THURSDAY, July 19th.

Commence Deck Tournaments ... ... 10-30 a.m.
Orchestra, Main Companion ... ... 11-0 a.m.
"Tote" on Ship's Run, "A" Deck Aft 11-0 to 12 Noon
Gymkhana, Sun Deck Aft ... ... 2-30 p.m.
Orchestra, Main Companion ... ... 4-0 p.m.
Carnival Dinner (Costume) ... 6-30 & 7-45 p.m.

FRIDAY, July 20th.

Arrive **Trondheim** ... ... 8-0 a.m.
Leave **Trondheim** ... ... 10-0 p.m.
Dancing, on Deck ... ... 9-0 p.m.

SATURDAY, July 21st.

Deck Tournaments continued ... ... 10-30 a.m.
Orchestra, Main Companion ... ... 11-0 a.m.
"Tote" on Ship's Run, ... 11-0 to 12 Noon
Arrive **Oie** ... ... 1-0 p.m.
Arrive **Hellesylt** ... ... 6-0 p.m.
Arrive **Merok** ... ... 8-0 p.m.
Dancing, on Deck ... ... 9-0 p.m.

SUNDAY, July 22nd.

Divine Service in Main Lounge ... ... 11-0 a.m.
Leave **Merok** ... ... 5-0 p.m.
Bridge Drive in "D" Deck Lounge ... 9-0 p.m.
Cinema in Main Lounge ... 7-30 & 9-40 p.m.
Dancing on Deck ... ... 9-0 p.m.

MONDAY, July 23rd.

Deck Tournaments continued ... ... 10-30 a.m.
Arrive **Gudvangen** ... ... 12-0 Noon
Leave **Gudvangen** ... ... 7-0 p.m.
Whist Drive, in "D" ... ... 9-0 p.m.
Dancing on Deck ... ... 9-0 p.m.

TU...

Arrive **Mundal**
Leave **Mundal**
Arrive **Balholm**
Dancing on Deck
Leave **Balholm**

WE...

Arrive **Bergen**
Leave **Bergen**
Orchestra, Main C...
INFORMAL CONCE...

Right: A selection of views of *Doric's* interior in 1934, showing just how much less opulent these cruise liners were than the earlier transatlantic vessels.

NO. 17
SHIP ASCANIA
DATE 12/2/48

CUNARD WHITE STAR LIMITED.

PASSENGER'S NAME SCOTT MR A

EXCHANGE VOUCHER.

$ 20-00 @ 4/10 £ 4-16-8

67/547.

B
10 ON
6 1 8
7 5 3

Left: **The Liverpool home of Captain E. J. Smith, the White Star Line's most famous skipper who perished in command of the *Titanic*.**

Below: **The Liverpool home of Thomas Henry Ismay. The owner's initials cast into the veranda supports (inset) and the commemorative plaque identify the building.**

ENGLISH HERITAGE
THOMAS
HENRY
ISMAY
1837-1899
Founder of the
White Star
Shipping Line
lived here

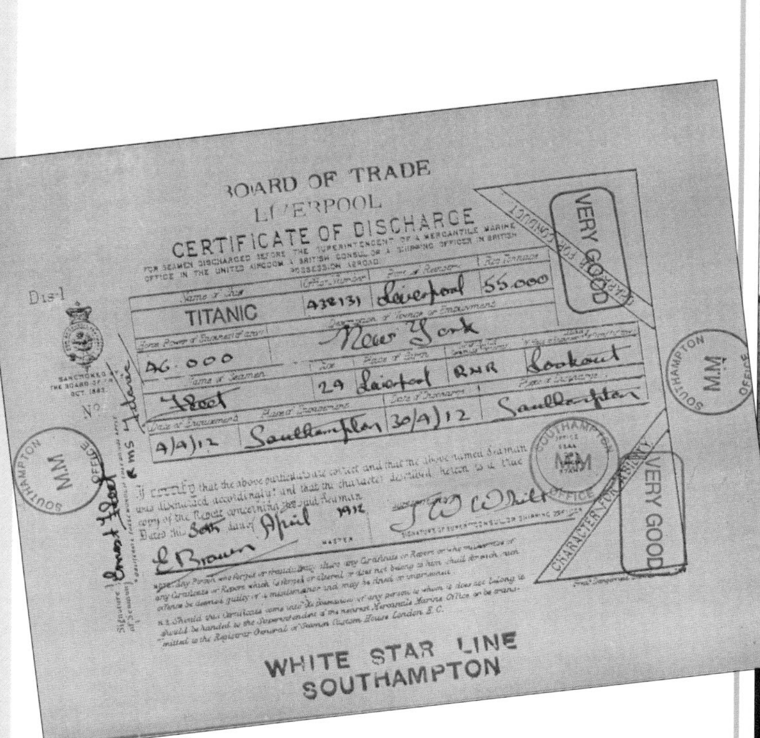

BOARD OF TRADE
LIVERPOOL
CERTIFICATE OF DISCHARGE
FOR SEAMEN DISCHARGED BEFORE THE SUPERINTENDENT OF A MERCANTILE MARINE OFFICE IN THE UNITED KINGDOM A BRITISH CONSUL OR A SHIPPING OFFICER IN BRITISH POSSESSION ABROAD

Dis 1

Name of Ship	Official Number	Port of Registry	Reg. Tonnage
TITANIC	438131	Liverpool	55.000

Horse Power of Engines (if any)	Description of Voyage or Employment
46.000	New York

Name of Seaman	Age	Place of Birth		Capacity
Fleet	29	Liverpool	RNR	Lookout

Date of Engagement	Place of Engagement	Date of Discharge	Place of Discharge
4/4/12	Southampton	30/4/12	Southampton

I certify that the above particulars are correct and that the above named Seaman was discharged accordingly and that the character described hereon is a true copy of the Report concerning the said Seaman.
Dated this 30th day of April 1912

E Brown
MASTER

J W White
SIGNATURE OF SUPERINTENDENT CONSUL OR SHIPPING OFFICER

Signature of Seaman: Ernest Fleet RMS Titanic

VERY GOOD
CHARACTER FOR CONDUCT

VERY GOOD
CHARACTER FOR ABILITY

SOUTHAMPTON M.M. OFFICE

WHITE STAR LINE
SOUTHAMPTON

Above: An example of a modern facsimile copy of a *Titanic* crewmember's discharge certificate.

Below: The Liverpool waterfront as it appears today, with the White Star Line office still standing.

Above: Majestic[2] in Southampton's Ocean Dock in the 1930s.

Below: A Cunard-White Star luggage label, showing *Queen Mary*.

Right: Song sheet from the 'Scholar's Cruise' of *Doric*[2] in mid-August 1933.

Far right: Another example of a modern copy of a White Star document; this time an account of wages. One wonders how easily these modern copies will be distinguished from the real thing before too long a time has passed.

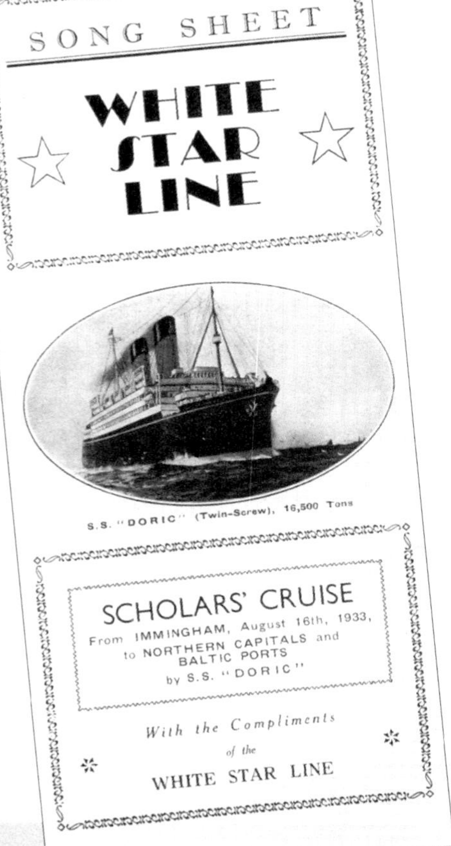

SONG SHEET
WHITE STAR LINE
S.S. "DORIC" (Twin-Screw), 16,500 Tons
SCHOLARS' CRUISE
From IMMINGHAM, August 16th, 1933, to NORTHERN CAPITALS and BALTIC PORTS by S.S. "DORIC"
With the Compliments of the
WHITE STAR LINE

F.

Issued by the BOARD OF TRADE, In pursuance of 57 & 58 Vict. ch. 60.

M. 12451.
1906.

ACCOUNT OF WAGES.

Name of Ship and Official Number	Name of Master.	Description of Voyage or Employment.
TITANIC	E J Smith	New York

Name of Seaman.	Reference No. in Agreement.	Date and Port of Engagement.	Date of Discharge.	Rate of Wages.
J Bailey	A/B	0/4/12 Southampton	15/4/12	£3 15/-

	Amount.			Deductions.	Amount.
Wages:— for ___ months 6 days....		15		Advance......	
[illegible]	1	12	6	Allotment	
	2	7	6	Fines and Forfeitures....	
Deductions as per contra..........					
Balance Due..............£	2	7	6	Total Deductions......£	

SOUTHAMPTON MM OFFICE

Dated at the Port of Southampton

this 30th day of April 30 APR 1912 SOUTHAMPTON C W Davenport for (Signature of Master.)

NOTICE TO MASTERS.—One of these Accounts must be filled up and delivered to each Member of the Crew, or if he is to be paid off at the Mercantile Marine Office, to the Superintendent of that Office, at least Twenty-four Hours before he is paid off, under a penalty not exceeding £5, and no deductions will be allowed unless duly inserted.

[391] Wt. 19751-135. 100,000. 10 11. W.H.S & S., N. Sch. 5. [Turn over.

WHITE STAR LINE
SOUTHAMPTON

PASSENGER
LIST.

CRUISE OF
S. S. "DORIC".
MADEIRA · PORTUGAL · SPAIN
JULY 15TH. TO JULY 27TH. 1933.

Right: **Front cover of the passenger list from *Doric*[2] for her July 1933 cruise to the Iberian peninsula.**

INDEX

***Below: Cedric* anchored in the Mersey.**

Above: *Ionic*[2] at anchor.